Thom Scheele

CATHARINE H. MURRAY lives with her two sons in Portland, Maine, where she teaches English to refugees and leads workshops on grief writing. She has read at Harvard University, Maine Medical Center, University of New England, and Maine State Prison. Murray earned her MFA at the Stonecoast Writing Program at the University of Southern Maine, where she was the creative nonfiction editor of the *Stonecoast Review*. *Now You See the Sky* is her first book.

Catherine Sebastian

Now You See the Sky is the debut selection of **ANN HOOD**'s new nonfiction imprint with Akashic, **Gracie Belle**. Modeled after her experience writing the memoir *Comfort: A Journey Through Grief*, and named after her daughter Grace, Hood's imprint reaffirms for authors and readers that none of us is alone in our journeys. She is the author of the best-selling novels *The Obituary Writer*, *The Knitting Circle*, and *The Book That Matters Most*. Hood was born in West Warwick, Rhode Island, and currently lives in Providence, Rhode Island. She is the editor of *Providence Noir*.

NOW YOU SEE THE SKY

NOW YOU SEE THE SKY

BY CATHARINE H. MURRAY

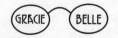

Published by Gracie Belle/Akashic Books
©2018 Catharine H. Murray

Trade Paperback ISBN-13: 978-1-61775-666-5
Library of Congress Control Number: 2018931655

All rights reserved
First printing

Gracie Belle
c/o Akashic Books
Brooklyn, New York
Twitter: @AkashicBooks
Facebook: AkashicBooks
E-mail: info@akashicbooks.com
Website: www.akashicbooks.com

Give sorrow words. The grief that does not speak
Whispers the o'erfraught heart and bids it break.
　　　—William Shakespeare, *Macbeth* (IV, iii)

To all those living with loss.
May you find a way to let your grief speak.

PART 1

RIVER

I T WAS SEPTEMBER 1989, the end of the rainy season, when the Mekong runs quick and mighty, flooding its banks and carrying huge limbs, sometimes whole trees, off like plunder. A dangerous flow of flotsam and force, the river is said to harbor, below the surface, a serpent-monster, especially greedy this time of year.

I didn't know that then. Twenty-three years old, jet-lagged, and knowing next to nothing about Thailand, I had arrived from my home in Maine only a week before. There I stood, in a line of searchers holding hands with other young volunteers—Japanese, Thai, British, and Canadians, who, like me, had come to work at the nearby refugee camp.

We were searching for a body.

The day before, a young man had left the confines of the camp to come here. Had he come to swim or to look back toward the land he pined for?

They found his shirt and trousers folded on the shore.

We stepped into the fast-moving river, so cloudy with silt that our feet glowed ghostly apparitions before vanishing from sight. The ceaseless current slurred any words in my head so that I kept silent, only wading in deeper, feet questioning riverbed with every step.

On the other side, half a mile across, fringes of jungle treetops sagged in the glare of midday sun. At our backs, mudbanks—heat-baked hard as stone that sometimes crumbled underfoot—rose up under a cluster of bamboo, wood, and thatch houses gathered at the river's edge.

The fierce sun burned our cheeks and beaded the sweat on our necks as we advanced. To the left, the river stretched west and then north to Tibet; to the right, it rolled east and south through Cambodia to the sea. Swirling water cooled backs of knees, thick of thighs, as we walked, slow with searching, hoping and dreading to feel something other than mud underfoot.

It seemed odd to me then that if we did find the boy's body, we would be giving the grieving mother what she most wanted and most feared.

~~

NEW HOME

~~

A WEEK EARLIER, I woke with my head against the cool glass window of the bus that carried me overnight from the airport in Bangkok to this northeastern edge of the country. I rubbed my eyes and looked out, the curiosity that had brought me waking me at once to a world as far from my own home as I could get.

On either side, a patchwork of rice paddies spread shimmering, reflecting lavender and gold of early-morning pastel skies. Brown water buffaloes leaned hulking bodies forward on spindly legs knee-deep in rainy-season mud, and a wavy line of blue hills stretched northward, all the way to our destination, a small town on the edge of the Mekong River, the border between Thailand and Laos.

As I marveled, I wondered what kind of place I had come to, so far from my New England home and the ivy-covered walls of the college I had finally graduated from, escaped. At last my life was my own, and I was ready to really learn.

The bus sank and rose through puddles in potholes, rocking us into town, and pulled up next to a bustling market. Tattered umbrellas tilted over squares of cloth laden with piles of fruits and vegetables I'd never seen. Over each, a female vendor presided, arranging her wares or laughing or arguing with the women around her.

I staggered sleepily off the bus where a crowd of men, drivers eager for business, pressed in close but did not touch me. I chose the nearest *tuk-tuk*, a motorcycle with a covered cart built onto the back, climbed in, and lifted my bags onto the polished aluminum floor. The driver looked at me, his face questioning as he realized I spoke no Thai. I repeated the phrase I had committed to memory before leaving home, "*Suk Somboon*," until he understood the name of the hotel where I wanted to go, where my new landlord would give me the key to the house I had arranged to rent. As he twisted the throttle to pull his machine out into the street, I held tight to the chrome bars behind me and looked around at this place that would be my home for a year, two at the most, I thought. "*Suk Somboon*." I didn't know then what it meant: Perfect Happiness.

Looking at the houses, I was disappointed not to see huts with thatched roofs perched on stilts under papaya trees, elephants striding by. Instead, two-story wooden buildings jostled for space on each side of the busy street. Men, women, and children strolled up and down, dressed in neatly ironed, pale yellow or pink or blue pajamas, chatting with neighbors, as nonchalant as if they were fully dressed. Women traced graceful arcs with short grass brooms, sweeping dust from the street in front of their houses as if the thoroughfare was as much theirs as the floors of the house behind them. Men smoked their first cigarettes of the day.

The sound of creaking and banging drew my attention to the houses where people unbolted and unfolded, accordion-style, hinged panels that made up the whole front walls of their houses, to be neatly split and collected at both corners of the buildings. I couldn't imagine exposing my home, my life like that.

At the end of the street, a quarter-mile from the bus stop, beyond an empty yard, lay an expanse of flat blue-gray water. The Mekong River.

The driver swung the tuk-tuk left around the corner, cut the engine, and I looked up to see my new home. Two-story, with boards gray from years of hard heat and rain, the house looked to me like all the rest.

I handed the driver a silver coin with a copper center. He slipped it into the pouch belted at his hip before kicking his bike back to life and leaving me and my bags by the door. I looked toward the hotel across the street, where wooden railings, dry and faded blue, trimmed the upstairs balconies above the street. From the cool darkness underneath, a short woman, top-heavy like a peahen, called to me.

She stepped into the light of the morning, already rising to a whiter glare than minutes before, hurried across the empty street, and, pulling a bunch of keys from her pocket, unlocked the heavy brass padlock and folded the door panel back on its hinges. I stepped over the threshold and breathed in the quiet stillness of the house. Then, following her example, I took off my shoes and walked behind her up the stairs.

A stream of unintelligible words flowed from her as she gestured first to the windows then the furniture, a heavy wooden table and two chairs with cushions. Dumb without her language, I could only smile and nod to show

I was delighted with the place and the furnishings. I followed her through a flimsy aluminum screen door into the small bedroom, closing it quickly before the mosquitoes could dart in behind us. I had read in my guidebook on the plane that Dengue fever was common.

Against the wall of thin unpainted plywood, a folding cot stood on rusty legs. On top lay a thin pad, sections tightly packed with feathery puffs from the pods of the kapok tree. On the opposite wall, a screened window with bars but no glass afforded an expansive view of corrugated tin roofs below in various stages of rust. Under my feet, the wide unvarnished floorboards shone with the polishing of decades of footsteps and scrubbings with oily halves of fresh coconut.

Someone else might have been disappointed in the austere furnishings. But I was delighted. It was my own place. Finally, I could live alone. I could enjoy quiet. No one to bother me. No one to interrupt me. No one to please. When I came home from work, I'd be able to write in my journal, write letters. Be quiet. After all the striving and endless talking and listening of eighteen years of school, I was at last in a world of my own, without language, without understanding. I could simply be.

I wanted to collapse on the bed to sleep. But even this far north of Bangkok, even in the rainy season, fifteen yards from the Mekong River and a half-mile from the jungles of Laos, it was hot and I was sticky. I needed a bath.

The smiling woman led me down the stairs and out the back door of the house to the bath area. Two doors of corrugated tin nailed to rotting wooden frames hung side by side. They opened onto dark, low rooms built of unpainted cinder block walls and smooth cement floors with only enough space to stand or squat. Behind the first door a long rectangular cement tank, chest-high, was built into half the space. It was filled with cold water from a single spigot. Even without words, I could read the woman's body language as she opened and closed the spigot so that only one drop of water at a time fell. I understood that I would need to be careful to keep plenty of water in the tank by leaving the spigot always dripping. The water was needed for bathing and, more importantly, flushing.

A lightbulb hung from the ceiling by its cord, and the woman dried her hands carefully before flicking the switch on the wall, as the exposed wiring was not well-insulated. I would soon develop the habit of using my elbow, a reliably dry body part, to turn wall switches on and off.

The toilet was new to me. A shiny porcelain oval bowl sunk right into the cement floor, its edges on two sides wider for the feet. The woman, with her experience cleaning at the Perfect Happiness hotel, was used to foreigners unfamiliar with Thai toilets. She knew how to handle this. Stepping across the toilet, she squatted to demonstrate the proper orientation for elimination. Then the flush lesson.

She picked up the thin red plastic bowl floating on the surface of the water, dipped one edge to fill it, then poured the water from shoulder height. The water swirled and burbled in the toilet, and I could see that her approach would be effective in a nonsimulated situation.

She then splashed several more bowls full of water all around the floors to clean up any imaginary splatters. In such hot, humid weather, this would be important to keep the bathroom smelling clean. She didn't seem to mind wasting water. With a whole river just beyond my doorstep, I guessed there was plenty.

"The important thing," a friend would later explain when we were discussing the finer points of bathing, "is that you never touch the water in the tank with your hands. Use the bowl to dip up the water because you don't want to contaminate water that might have to be used for cooking or tea. And don't let the bowl sink." I imagined having to step into the dark cold water to retrieve a sunken bowl and shuddered.

COMMUTE

AFTER A WEEK OF WAITING for my paperwork to be sent from the Catholic Offices of Emergency Relief and Refugees in Bangkok, I started work at the camp. It was a one-hour commute from the town where we lived to the camp fifty-six kilometers downriver. In the backseat of the minivan each morning, I gazed at the green jungles of Laos on the other side of the river, a sight that changed each day with light and season. I never tired of the commute before and after a hectic day of work.

In that first month, I learned from my Thai coworkers enough of the language to haggle with tuk-tuk drivers and market women. After weekdays spent in the refugee camp, trying to tame the rules of English grammar for the two dozen Hmong staff who taught the children and teenagers of the camp of 42,000 refugees, I needed the quiet of the ride. For most of the teachers, English was not their second language, as I had assumed when I first arrived. Many spoke not only Hmong, Thai, and Laotian, but Chinese, Russian, and French as well. All day words buzzed past my ears in lines of sound with rhythms and tones unique to each language. Some of it I tried to understand and remember.

I was surprised by how much I loved this, my first real job. In leaving home to follow the do-gooder's dream of teaching in a refugee camp, I had thought I was coming to teach poor, backward people. As a bright young American, educated in the best schools, I had been taught to believe that I held the key to success for the "less fortunate" people of the world.

I wasn't long in the camp before I realized I might have gotten that wrong. In trying to learn the ways of the new cultures I was in—Hmong, Lao, and Thai—I began to feel like *I* was the backward one, the uncivilized one. I noticed the way the teachers in the camp and the people around me in the town took such care with simple tasks—erasing a chalk board, wiping deep into each corner, stepping through a door, ironing a shirt—and the way they paid close, calm attention when I spoke.

Riding home in the van a few months after starting work at the camp, I was absorbing the peace that the view of hazy curves of the Mekong offered, and I realized the daily commute would be perfect for biking, I wrote to my mother asking her to send my road bike back with a friend who was coming to Thailand to work.

It arrived at the end of the rainy season.

~~

MEETING

~~

I HAD BEEN WORKING IN THE CAMP for a year when one night my friends and I walked into the small restaurant where we usually ate, a collection of rickety tables set up on the first floor of a modest house. In front of the house, the owner presided over her section of the street, cooking at her huge wok, caked underneath with layers of black sooty grease, but gleaming silver inside. Beside it stood a glass case with plucked chickens and ducks hanging by their throats. Customers greeted her and gave their orders as they walked in before making themselves at home in front of her television.

That night a group of Thai men sat by the far wall. One of my friends walked over to talk with them. He called me over and introduced me to the one he knew by name. I immediately felt the familiar sense of superiority and judgment I often experienced when I saw groups of men together like this. In the year I'd been there, I'd noticed rudeness only from drunken men. Sober, they would have barely acknowledged me and kept their distance, but drunk, they always smiled too eagerly and called out, "Byootifun! Byootifun!" waiting for some response. I always returned a glare. I concluded that many Thai men simply drank too much. The empty bottles of Mekong whiskey on the table beside the half-eaten plates of food and bowls of soup indicated that these men were no different.

But they looked different. Wearing clothes reminiscent of American cowboys, tight jeans, denim jackets, cowboy shirts with snaps, and leather vests, these men did not look like any I had encountered in this small town so far. Almost all the other men I'd met here wore their hair in neat crew cuts, but these had long hair, pulled back in unruly ponytails or tucked behind their ears. The one I'd been introduced to had hair that hung long and loose, silky and black over the back of a leather bomber jacket worn to softness and covered with an eclectic collection of patches. When we met, he turned his gaze to me, and I was surprised to find myself pulled into the warmth of an open and inviting smile. He politely offered his hand in the Western style, not waiting for me to bow respectfully, as a woman meeting a man not obviously younger should have. He then introduced me to each of his rowdy friends. I didn't think anything of it.

A few days later, I was riding home from work in the back of the minivan. It was October, the end of the rainy season. We were curving around a particularly scenic bend when I spotted a cyclist who'd stopped to take in the view.

"Hey, look, there's that guy we saw the other night. I told you he was a biker," my friend said to me. I remembered. In the moment that we sped past, I took it all in: his sleek road bike, his figure looking out over the river, the fact that his round-trip bike ride would be over sixty miles, and that he had incredible legs.

* * *

A week later, I was riding alone after a dusty day at work to clear my head and take in the beauty of the hills and river at sunset when I saw the same longhaired cyclist jogging on the road ahead. I had no interest in a romance, but I did think a riding buddy would be nice. As I pulled up behind him, I noticed his sweat-drenched shoulders and the curves of his calf muscles on legs that bowed like a lobsterman's. I slowed to his pace and said hello.

Immediately his face, drawn in concentration and effort, brightened into that magnetic smile. I offered him some water from my bottle, which he politely refused twice before I convinced him to have some. He kept up his pace while he tilted back his head and put the worn plastic spout between his lips. I was amazed anyone could sweat that profusely, but on his smooth skin it only looked inviting. In as off-hand a manner as I could manage, I started a conversation, asking him about his biking routine. He didn't speak much English, and I spoke even less Thai, so our conversation was short. I said goodbye and rode off ahead.

When I was returning in near darkness, I was surprised to look up at the bridge into town, not far from where I'd met this man, to find him standing next to his bike, facing me, waiting. He smiled and mounted his bike to join me for the ride back to town. We chatted a bit more and reintroduced ourselves. We decided to meet the next night to play badminton on the local court.

Dtaw. A hard name to pronounce, like so many others here. I shrugged inwardly. No matter. He was just someone to bike and exercise with. But he did have a nice smile.

BADMINTON

*D*TAW PICKED ME UP ON HIS WHITE MOTORBIKE. I sat well behind him, straddling the large seat. A Thai woman my age would have sat side-saddle in a similar situation, but I couldn't bear to be so prim. We rode through town until he stopped and pressed the kickstand down in front of one of the weather-worn wooden buildings on the main street. He led me down a narrow alley to a thin wooden door. Stepping over the high threshold, built to keep out snakes, our footsteps echoed under the high ceilings of what used to be the town's only movie theater. As we walked inside and Dtaw found the light switch easily in the dark, I saw that most of the rows of folding wooden seats had been removed. Faded dust-covered velvet drapes still hung in tattered strips from the tops of the tall walls all around.

Dtaw led me out onto the clean-swept wooden floor and handed me the racket he'd packed into a bright Dunlop bag for me. The racket gleamed with city slickness and felt light and springy in my hand. As we stood by the tightly strung net next to the rusty high chair for the line judge, Dtaw held my hand loosely around the racket's grip, teaching me how to hold it correctly. I noticed his muscular hands and graceful fingers ending in clean well-trimmed nails.

He walked to his side of the net and lobbed a few shots over for me to return. I did okay, I thought, flailing at the light birdies. Every now and then I walked back to the edge of the net between us, using body language to ask him to help me readjust my grip, and every time, his soft palms and slender, strong fingers wrapped gently around mine as he smiled and showed me what I wanted.

After a while Dtaw's friends arrived and began rallying shots on the court next to us. Though I couldn't understand what they were saying as they chattered at him and he laughed along, it was clear that they were teasing him about his *farang* guest. Foreigners, or *farang* as the locals say, were not a rarity in the village. There were at least a dozen of us working in the refugee camp, and with the town's strategic location across the river from Laos, there had been a foreign presence there since the beginning of the Vietnam War, though a Thai-farang couple was unusual.

Soon it was time for them to compete. I folded down one of the wooden seats from the front row and settled in to watch. The game was fast, and the portly, middle-aged players in cheap, thin-soled sneakers were surprisingly quick and agile as they lunged for shots it seemed they couldn't possibly reach but almost always did. They laughed and shouted as they played, but there was no question about the intensity of their concentration and competition. I was transfixed.

There was also no question as to which player dominated the court. Dtaw lunged and fired shots so fast that the white-feathered bullet blurred in my sight as it shot across the net. But most amazing were his slams. Each time the birdie arched high overhead, Dtaw crouched, coiling to spring into a sudden curve of power, stopping the projectile's descent and sending it, impossible to intercept, to his opponent's feet. If the vision alone wasn't terrifying to his opponent, the loud grunt of power issued with each swat would have been. As I watched this perfection of form, I realized I was noticing also breadth of shoulders and beauty of arms as they reached at every opportunity.

When I left the court to walk home, I felt spacey as I noticed the warm yellow glow of lights coming from the houses where people shushed babies and washed dinner dishes. I heard the hum of the crickets in my quiet lane and the boards of my porch squeak under my bare feet. I lifted the heavy padlock from the hasp screwed into the door and felt the clean cool of the polished planks underfoot. I walked into my room, dropped my clothes to the floor, and slid under the gauzy white mosquito net to lie down and dream.

~~

FALLING

~~

*I*N THE LATE AFTERNOON A FEW DAYS LATER, I was waking up from the after-work sleep that the motion of the minivan often induced as we rode home from work. We were pulling up to our first stop at the edge of town. Outside the window, Dtaw stood smiling next to his motorbike, waiting. In each hand, he held an ice cream cone. I looked, unbelieving, as he nodded to me to get out of the van. He had come to pick me up. I felt my face burning at the teasing of my coworkers as I stepped to the door. I licked the sweet surprise, delicious in the heat and still frozen enough to resist my bites.

After a few more evenings of biking and badminton followed by dinner at the restaurant where we'd met, I began to notice things about this man. I marked the way he selected special morsels of food from his plate, gently placing them onto mine, the way everyone in town knew him and smiled at him approvingly whenever we met them, the way he spoke to children.

I decided it would be safe to get closer to him. I had no notion of anything like a long-term or even committed relationship. I was twenty-three and tired of sleeping alone each night. I knew I'd be leaving in eight months to go home, my two-year adventure in a foreign land drawing to a close. In my mind, he was only a playmate, a face, a story to add to the experience of living in an exotic world I'd impress my friends with when I got home.

Because our language was limited, I relied on my observations of his actions. Not a big talker, especially about himself, he never would have told me all the things I noticed. When I accompanied him on his frequent visits to his grandparents' house, I watched the tenderness and reverence with which he helped them cook their meals, sweep their floors, even clip their toenails, all in such a way as befitted their dignity and the honor with which he regarded them. I watched them touch the top of his head, smiling at him, as he sat, crouched at their feet, and saw the approval, the appreciation in those small gestures.

When we did talk, when were able to understand each other with the few words we shared, the things he told me painted a picture of a man who'd grown up with an abundance of love from his family and devotion from his friends. He told me about his gang, boys his age who'd made their own rebellious adventures through childhood and still stuck together as adults. He told me stories that made me laugh or gasp with shock. When he was ten, he and his friends wanted to go *pai teeo*, out for fun. He told his friends to pile into the dusty truck bed. He slid in behind the wheel for the first time in his life, and off they rode, laughing and hollering as they waved to the neighbors on their way to the farm.

He had this great sense of fun, but he was also deeply disciplined. He told me about getting up at four o'clock each morning as a middle school student, long before the rest of his siblings, to train for badminton. He ran along the river, sprinting and practicing his footwork to perfect his performance. Then he'd go get the key from the owner of the court so he could practice alone for an hour with the basket of old shuttlecocks he'd collected to perfect his serve. His hard work paid off. By his sophomore year in high school he had won the provincial championship title and was invited to train in Bangkok with players from the national team. His determination and discipline impressed me.

He seemed resourceful too. By the time he was eight years old, he'd set up a drink stand at the court where his father and his friends played badminton in the evenings. There he'd sell bottles of Coke and Sprite and Fanta he'd bought for four baht each. He charged five baht and took home the profits. He always had spending money for candy he'd share with his friends.

When he graduated from high school and all his older siblings were pursuing their college diplomas, his mother sold her last pieces of gold jewelry to send him to Bangkok to do the same. That didn't last. A back injury he'd sustained from a fall in badminton years earlier kept him from sitting for long periods, so listening to lectures wasn't for him. Instead he was always moving, seeing friends, which at that age meant drinking. He told me stories of back-alley gambling and brawls, the last one of which landed him in the hospital and brought his father to his bedside in Bangkok to tend him until he was well enough to go home for good. I was learning that this quiet, respectful man who played like a little kid with his toddler nieces had a bad-boy streak.

When Dtaw invited me to take a short bike trip with

him to the mountains, I said yes. One of Dtaw's lifelong friends, Cam, had moved to a village a few hundred kilometers west of their home when they were in their twenties. Another friend had wanted to introduce Cam to a village girl there. Twelve years his junior, Tong was strong, hardworking, and kind. In her world, being fifteen and marrying a twenty-seven-year-old man was not unusual or unwise. They married and moved into her mother's house to help with the farm until they could build their own place.

Dtaw wanted to take me to visit them. We biked past mango groves, rubber tree farms, the green and golden hills rolling away under our tires. The last ten kilometers up the mountain to their village was hard, but I loved the challenge. When we got close to the village, we had to cross a stream where the bridge was nothing more than a few thick tree trunks laid side by side across it. At the top of the rutted dirt road to the bridge, I had to stop and gather my courage before making the commitment to cross, knowing one wrong twist of the handlebars or falter in my pedal stroke and I would fall hard, maybe into the rocky stream below. I chanted to myself as my bicycle bounced over the rough road and I gathered speed toward the crude, treacherous bridge: *No fear. No fear. No fear.* I pressed my jaw tight to keep from banging my teeth when my tires hit the skinned trees. *No fear. No fear. No fear.* I held the handlebars steady, standing on the pedals, knees bent to let the bike bounce beneath me, keeping my eyes on ground. And I was across.

The village was so remote that people in front of their homes stopped in midmotion to stare at these strange visitors in bright lycra clothes with bulging packs attached to their bikes. When we rolled to a stop in front of Tong and Cam's house, people clustered around us, asking what we had come to sell. The outsiders who came to the village were usually traveling salespeople.

Cam came out to welcome us, explaining to his neighbors who we were, and invited us to sit in the shade in front of his hut. He called to Tong, and she appeared as well. She was silent, too shy to look up, but she returned with a bottle of drinking water and two glasses before retreating into the safety of her home.

Dtaw took me down to the narrow stream below the garden so we could bathe. As bathing in the village was not a private event, he showed me how to wear one of the sarongs he had asked Cam to get from Tong. Wearing it as I stood on the sand under the clean moving water, I dipped my body below the surface and took the soap he handed me. When I got out, he helped me slip a dry sarong over my head before removing the wet one from underneath.

Over the night and day that followed, I grew used to being in a place without running water, without electricity, only flickering flames to light the way at night. I loved the quiet, the simplicity. I loved the way the neighbors gathered around the fire to talk at night after dinner while the children ran and played together. I loved the rough boards of the floor under my bare feet as I sat and watched Tong prepare meals.

Behind her two-room hut, a smaller structure that was the kitchen stood connected to the first by a board suspended over the mud. A square of dried mud was built into the center of the floor to serve as a fireplace. It was here that Tong cooked. Sitting beside the fire, she had everything within reach from the narrow shelves Cam had built into the walls. She never let me help her with the kitchen work. I sat, just wanting to be near her, another woman. Without words in each other's language, we found communication in looks and smiles alone.

After a few days in this village, a place that seemed idyllic to me in my quest for quiet, in my desire to escape my own industrialized world, it was time to return to work. We said goodbye, promising we'd soon return. When we left, our packs were heavy with fresh melons and squashes and other gifts of the fields and gardens from Tong and her neighbors.

In the weeks that followed, Dtaw and I became closer, jogging and playing badminton together, taking walks by the river, losing ourselves in one another's gaze, finding reasons to laugh and kiss. I kept telling him that this was playful short-term love. I would be going home soon, I assured him. Yet even as I tried to convince myself of this, I began to have visions of the two of us together, as old as his grandparents. I liked these visions. For the first time, never having been interested in commitment or progeny, I found myself imagining life as a grandmother of numerous kids with this smiling, easygoing man. It was this vision, more than anything else, that drew me even closer to Dtaw and began to open my mind to the possibility of a long-term relationship. I began to see that the qualities he possessed—patience, integrity, depth, and reticence— might not be easily found in another man.

~~

LAND

~~

A YEAR AFTER OUR FIRST VISIT TO CAM AND TONG, I left my job at the refugee camp. I had worked for the two years I'd planned on, and as the Thai government made more of an effort to resettle or repatriate the refugees, many of my friends had gone back home to their own countries. As I fell deeper in love with Dtaw, leaving him each morning to go to work became less tolerable. There was always plenty of other work in town for a native English speaker with teaching experience. To support myself, I ran a small after-school English class; we would meet at the table under the shady mango tree in Dtaw's yard. The fact that Dtaw's family was so well-known and well-respected in town gave me instant clout and a long waiting list for the classes. I couldn't charge much, but having survived on $200 a month as a teacher in the refugee camp, I was used to living simply. Dtaw's family seemed to delight in feeding us sumptuous meals every time we stopped by his mother's or grandmother's house. We could have eaten well anywhere. In Thailand the first greeting is not "Hello, how are you?" but "Have you eaten yet? Come eat with us." People genuinely welcome friends and acquaintances to share food at every meal. In the Buddhist mind, generosity is a privilege and a pleasure.

Our low-income, low-effort lifestyle meant we could focus on time together. So when Dtaw suggested we go for another visit to Cam and Tong in the mountains, I agreed immediately.

When we arrived, Cam told us he wanted to show us the land he had recently acquired from a neighbor. The next morning we rose in the dark to eat sun-dried pork Tong heated over the coals between sticks of bamboo, secured with twists of bamboo skin. A chorus of crickets and peepers filled the air as we dipped hunks of sticky rice in *geow*, a bright red paste of dried and roasted hot chilies, garlic, sugar, shallots, and salt. We spoke only a few words, enough to acknowledge Tong's work and skill. She picked up the dishes, and Cam and Dtaw and I stepped out the door and onto the earth under a sky the color of steel.

On the road in front of the hut, a group of neighbors gathered, men in wide-brimmed straw hats and long-sleeved ragged shirts. They smiled and greeted us, chatting as they waited for the fuel-powered plow to carry them to the fields that needed harvesting that day. Soon it came chugging up the road and they climbed onto the flatbed behind it.

They asked us where we were going. "To look at the land," Cam replied. No more words were needed. They knew Cam and the goings-on of his life well enough to know that he would be taking us to see the land on the mountain he'd recently acquired.

Following the only road up out of the village, we

walked away from the clink of breakfast dishes washed in
basins behind houses where chickens waited for scraps,
away from the barking dogs and squealing children preparing for school. As the road took us higher, Cam and
Dtaw chatted in low tones, each with a machete, sheathed
in smoke-darkened bamboo, hanging at his side. I walked
beside Dtaw, content to be somewhere quiet and cool at
last, spaciousness of sky and fields rolling away in every
direction. At the edges of the fields, yellowing as the sun
rose higher, green jungles fringed the ridges. Under our
feet the soft dust rose in puffs with every step.

After half a mile, we passed one of the King of Thailand's agricultural development centers, fenced in and
carefully tended, full of groves of fruits that had never
been seen in this area, macadamia nuts, avocados, cof-
fee. The king's mission in life was to better the lives of
his subjects, especially in the poorest areas of the country. He had spent much of his fifty-year career traveling
to remote villages where he asked questions, studied,
drew maps, and, most of all, listened to the farmers talk
about the challenges of their lives. Part of his solution
was to fund these centers, where local people were hired
to grow and study and teach about new crops that might
help bring better income to the villagers.

Cam led us through the gate to show us the different
trees and flowers that grew there. He told us that no one
liked the avocados, didn't know what to do with them,
had tried them mashed with sugar, but they did not take,
so piles were left to rot under the trees. He promised he'd
let me know when the next harvest came. I hadn't eaten
an avocado in the two years since I'd been in Thailand.

We walked through another gate and out onto the

road again where it curved around a small pond. Here a few fishermen stood up to their waists in the cold water, throwing wide round nets that spread out between the cobalt sky and gray-green surface, twine knotted in perfect webs, weighted at the edges with small stones crocheted into snug pockets. In splashing mandalas, the nets fell and the men pulled at the purse strings beneath to gather the edges and any fish that might be caught within.

"*Mahn baw?*" (Any luck?) Cam called out, using the special word *mahn*, reserved for asking about fishing. It also is the word for *pregnant*. "*Baw,*" they answered back.

We walked on, higher with each step, until on our left, a long ridge came into view above the tall grasses by the road. "*Hen baw?*" (You see?) Cam asked. "The land." In Laotian and Thai the words for *my* and *mine* are rarely used in conversation. The idea of ownership is much less embedded in the language and the collective mind. It is *the land* more than it is *Cam's land*. In a society living so close to the earth, the notion that the land belongs to any one person is foolish. The awareness that, instead, the people belong to the land, the land that provides everything they eat and drink and, until the last century, wear, is so much a part of them that they probably would think it odd to even try to discuss the concept. It might be the land where Cam plants his crops now, and people would acknowledge his ownership if necessary, but possessive pronouns do not exist in Thai and Lao. The words *of Cam* must be used to convey ownership. A cumbersome inconvenience.

We turned from the dust of the road and began the ascent to the ridge. Dense grass, taller than our heads and with edges that drew blood when they hit your skin at the wrong angle, slowed our walk even more. For this we had all worn long sleeves and sturdy trousers despite the warmth of the sun. I walked behind the men as they slashed a path with their machetes through this grass that had earned the name *Ya Ka*, or Communist grass. The grass got its name because during what is known to Americans as the Vietnam War, Communists were infiltrating Thailand and hiding in the jungles and mountains. The grass, like the Communists, increased rapidly where planted and no matter how many times it was cut down, it always came back. I hoped the commotion would scare away any cobras that might be nearby.

After a long climb, when the sweat began to trickle down my neck and the skin at my wrists itched from the stinging edges of the grass, we emerged into a yellow field of broken stalks at our feet. Above us the sky spread blue and vast as ahead of us the mountain dropped suddenly away into a valley, thirty kilometers across to where distant hills lined the horizon in blue waves. We walked across the field, listening to Cam talk about the black beans he'd plant in time to harvest before the next rice crop was sown.

Below us the long sloping wall of jungle fell, trees and vines growing thick and lush, harboring countless kinds of insects and reptiles and mammals. Tigers and elephants had not been seen here in the last couple of years. They were safer across the valley in the national park where the mountains were. Guards patrolled there to keep poachers from the big animals and the orchids. Orchid hunters came here to comb the jungle, and the villagers from here went there to hunt. The men we knew would not kill an elephant or tiger. They hunted for food, not for the international market. They brought wild boar, deer, anteaters, or mole rats home to feed their families and neighbors.

Cam pointed out a line of road that wandered across the valley floor and led to Tong's mother's village, a nineteen-kilometer walk that he and Tong and their three-year-old daughter made regularly. While Cam and Dtaw talked, I wandered down the ridge. Still not fluent in the language, I needed translation from Dtaw to keep up, and I sometimes had to interrupt him so he could explain things to me. Sometimes it was easier to be alone. I came to a grassy place like a small lawn that curved out above the jungle. In the middle of this clear space stood a freshly cut tree stump, hip high. I went to it and followed the urge to climb up and sit. As I settled myself cross-legged, feet resting on thighs, on the newly cut surface, I felt a quiet rush of stillness. I felt a clean emptiness.

In the past months I had become a student of Buddhism and meditation, and to sit and feel something that approached nothing was a thrill. I sat, enjoying the new sensation, gazing out at so much muted green and blue and spacious sky and earth. I sat for a long time. It wasn't until years later that I wondered if I had been the beneficiary of all those years of energy from the earth flowing into the trunk of the tree; perhaps the energy was still surging upward despite the tree being gone. I don't know the explanation, but I know that day I fell in love with that place, that piece of land. And in my childish desire for endless bliss, when I had climbed down from my perch, and Cam and Dtaw came walking down the path, I said to Dtaw, "Oh, can't we live here? Can't we just stay here forever? Do we ever have to leave?" He smiled, as usual, an answer without an answer.

CONSENT

*T*WO YEARS AFTER OUR FIRST DATE, I agreed to let Dtaw's parents host a spirit-calling ceremony before we left for the US. I said I would do it only if it was not a wedding. After three years living in Thai rural culture and two years living as an almost-member of Dtaw's family, I knew that the community looked at us as a married couple and would love to celebrate our union with a good wedding. Whether for a house raising, naming ceremony, wedding, or to end an illness, a spirit-calling ceremony varied only in the words spoken and the intentions of the hosts and guests. It always involved elders, a special sculpture of oiled and curled banana leaves, jasmine blossoms, chanting monks, crowds of neighbors, family and friends, and plenty of food and whiskey. Even though we'd applied for a fiancé visa for Dtaw after he'd been refused a tourist visa by the US consulate, I was not ready for a wedding. I had little faith in the institution of marriage, and I didn't see why our love needed government approval.

His parents had the invitations custom-printed with pink hearts. They consulted the seer for the most auspicious date and the right number of monks to attend. Dtaw's great-aunt provided the handwoven silk sarong and matching shoulder scarf she had worn for her own wedding. Dyed garnet, from the luminous nest of a wood-boring insect, and with intricate patterns of gold and black woven into the sparkling threads, it dazzled me, and I relented. I went to Dtaw's cousin, the best seamstress in the province, to be measured for a shirt of raw cream-colored silk, and prepared myself for a wedding.

That first year of marriage, I often wondered about living so far from home. I missed my friends, I missed speaking my language. I felt alone. Yet I also felt held, part of a strong web of community, each strand clearly defined by age and gender. I knew immediately when I was introduced to someone where I stood in relation to him or her. Each name was preceded by a word defining this. *Older brother, maternal aunt, great-grandmother, little sister, little child.* My own role as the young wife of a good man in a well-respected family was well-defined. I was meant to be a respectful, kind daughter-in-law, aunt, neighbor. And, in turn, I was shown respect and kindness from those around me. But I worried that this was not what I had been raised for. I was smart. I was a feminist. Was I wasting my skills and education here in this place so remote from my own people?

I was working—busy teaching at the local schools when their budgets allowed them to bring in a native English speaker for stints, and helping Dtaw run the small guest house he had turned our home into—but I still felt I needed to find my true calling.

I thought graduate school back in the US might be the

answer and began sending off for catalogs on dance ther-
apy programs. I read them and imagined our life in the
US where we would both work while I went to school. In
the midst of this planning and dreaming, I stood washing
dishes one afternoon, cool water running over my hands,
heat from the crackling hot tin roof warming the top of
my head. As I reminded myself to keep my mind on my
task, to sustain awareness of my current movements rather
than letting it wander, I realized I had been learning from
books since before kindergarten. I wanted now to learn
from life. I realized I did not want to go back to a world of
achievement and striving.

It wasn't that living in Thailand didn't require work.
Dtaw and I both worked, we both looked after the foreign
travelers who stayed in our home, and I taught English—but
the pressure to get ahead, to climb the career ladder, to be
a "success," was not there for me in Thailand as it always
had been in the US. This was partly because I felt anony-
mous. There was no one to impress or please as there was
at home. My identity in the eyes of the people in my community, beyond being Dtaw's wife, was simply being an
American. To them I already was a success. I had made it
karmically; I had found rebirth as a white US citizen, the
pinnacle of privilege and happiness. Their view of karma
offered a tacit support for the privilege I enjoyed despite
my awareness of it. It made it comfortable for me to rest
there. Living in Thailand allowed me to avoid the pressure I felt to do something impressive with my career.
I didn't think of all this consciously. I only knew that I
wanted to stay in this community, learning the lessons of
generosity and interconnected living that were all around
me. I wanted to have children with this man I loved and

raise them inside his big family with doting aunts and uncles and cousins and neighbors. I wanted my children to have the kind of childhood I did not.

Raised in a sterile affluent suburb of Chicago by a mom forced to work when her husband left her with two children under six, I had spent too many hours of my childhood alone. My companions after school most days were the characters I saw on television. *Gilligan's Island, The Brady Bunch, The Flintstones*. These imaginary people were more real to me than the neighbors in the houses on our street. In this safe, clean, quiet neighborhood, I had been lonely.

Now, in this small town by the river, loneliness dogged me too, but in a different way. I could always hear the neighbors through the thin walls of our houses, so close we could have reached our arms out the windows and touched. I could look down the lane to see the moving water of the river, alive and soft as a companion. I could look up the lane to the temple where the monks moved slow and steady, sweeping, chanting, listening. I could not really feel alone, even when I was lonely.

MOTHERHOOD

*I*WAS IN NO HURRY TO HAVE CHILDREN despite my dreams of grandparenting. It was three years after marriage before I got pregnant, and then it was not planned. But when my first son was born, I was shocked by the depth of maternal love that had been waiting to pour out of me with his body. Because it was my first baby, and I wanted a home birth, we flew home to Maine. I labored at home, but when our midwife Schyla realized he wasn't coming quick enough, she decided we needed to move to the hospital. He was born healthy and strong enough to return to Thailand at two months old.

Twelve days after Cody was born in the US, Dtaw's sister Jum gave birth to a little girl, Jew, at our local hospital in Thailand. Jum was the family's big-city businesswoman. She had lived in Bangkok since going to boarding school there before college. But Bangkok is no place to raise a baby, so, as so many young parents do in Thailand, she had long since planned to leave the baby with the grandmother to raise in the village, while she and her husband made money in the big city and prepared for when their child would live with them to attend school.

From the start of my pregnancy, I had hoped for twins and had dutifully eaten every pair of fused bananas I saw, as my neighbors told me if I did, I might have twins. With Jew's birth so close to Cody's, my wish had mostly come true. They spent every waking hour together. Every time we went to the market or for bike rides or walks, we took the two of them, and when people asked if they were twins, I always nodded yes.

I loved Jew. I nursed her at my breast beside Cody. I rocked the two in one big wicker basket suspended from the porch beams. I sang lullabies to them before they slept in the afternoons. Side by side, the babies sat in the big trailer behind my bike when Dtaw and I took evening rides along the Mekong. At home, Dtaw's mother and I kept each other company as we sat and watched the two of them while they napped, waving cloths over their bodies to keep the mosquitoes away from their tender skin.

MEI YA

EI YA MEANS PATERNAL GRANDMOTHER, and that is how I addressed my mother-in-law. She and I had plenty of time to talk during those years when Cody and Jew were little. Together, we sat for hours, swinging them in the bamboo cradle to keep them sleeping, watching them play in the clean-swept dirt of the yard, safe under the mango tree. Sometimes I asked her about her life. Judging from her replies, I don't think anyone else ever had. She'd raised five boys, Dtaw the fifth, and one girl, Jum, the last baby. As a mother, she had cultivated a fierce and effective vigilance. Despite dengue fever, malaria, poisonous snakes, and living only a few meters from the Mekong River with its greedy spirits and often fatally capricious currents, all her children survived, and all but one, my husband, the rebel, went to college in Bangkok, the city of refinement and money, a world away.

When we shared meals together at her table, her sons barely spoke. As far as I could see, only when they shared a bottle of beer or whiskey with other men did the talk begin and never falter, conversation clicking along, picking up speed, whirling around corners of phrases, tumbling through tunnels of laughter and stories. With their mother, though, they were mostly silent. Jum would address her with more familiarity, but still reverence. I did not ever hear Jum pose questions about her mother's past.

With me it was different. As the daughter-in-law and a foreigner, I was not only one step removed from the rules of the family, I was usually forgiven when I was oblivious to them. I was able to get away with what people within the culture would be blamed for as disrespectful. So I asked a lot of questions. What was it like, I wondered, to grow up in a dusty village on the Mekong River, to live through Japanese and American presence during two wars? What was it like to be a young mother in a place so remote that seeing a doctor required a two-day ride on the back of a plodding water buffalo through jungle where tigers waited for fresh meat to wander by? But more than these things, I wanted to know my mother-in-law's mind. I wanted to get past the fear and petty resentments and preoccupation with daily tasks of cooking and sweeping and laundry and hear about her inner world. So I asked more questions. And because I knew that the earliest experiences so strongly shape our psyches, I pressed her mostly about those.

One day, while the babies slept, she told me about the little brother she adored when she was a child. She doted on him, taking him everywhere with her and her other little sister. They would fight over who got to carry him and hold his hand. She bathed him and dressed him and fed him. At twelve, she was almost old enough to have her own children, and her mother was busy with all the work the house and farm and monks in the temple down the street required. So my mother-in-law mothered the little boy she loved.

He was six or seven when he was playing on the porch one day, she told me. He leaned against the railing, rotted from years of rain. Then he leaned too hard and fell through to the earth below where he lay still and silent. Panicked, Mei Ya ran to him, bending over him to find him alive, with only the wind knocked out of him. But after that, he grew sick and the fever came. His parents bathed him in cool water, muttered prayers over him, asked the monks to intervene, rubbed him with coins, and tied strings on his small wrists to call back the spirits that had gone wandering, leaving him sick and fading. Nothing worked. Day by day the infection spread until his skin became a solid bruise and he died.

As she told me this story, Jew and Cody lay next to each other, plump and clean, on the cotton quilts she'd sewn for them, under the safety of a mosquito net covering them like cakes in a Parisian bakery. The electric fan purred as it swung side to side, blowing the mosquitoes from us and keeping the babies cool in the afternoon heat. I watched her face, surprised and gratified to see her eyes moisten as she talked of her little brother's death. I didn't want to cause her sadness; I wanted her to heal from the hurt of those losses.

Later that night as Dtaw and I lay under our mosquito net, our baby asleep between us in the dark, I told him the story. He was quiet, then said, "I never knew about that." After a long silence: "I'd heard my grandmother had twelve children, ten of whom died. Whenever anyone asks her how many children she had, though, she always says two."

~~~

A PLACE ON THE MOUNTAIN

~~~

WHEN CODY WAS SIX MONTHS OLD, we returned again to Cam and Tong's village. It was early January, and in Thailand New Year's is the time for gift giving. "I have a present for you," Dtaw had told me as we prepared to leave our house by the river. "You'll see when we get there." I didn't think much of it. Dtaw wasn't big on gifts, so I didn't expect much.

The first morning after we'd arrived at Cam and Tong's, we again made the walk up from the village to the mountain. I carried Cody on my back and told him about everything we saw. When we passed the pond, Dtaw pointed to the ridge of Cam's new land. At the top sat a small brown square topped with a triangle. A new hut. I didn't think much of that either. Farmers were always building shelters for the planting and harvesting of a crop. They needed shade and sometimes a place to sleep. When we reached the top of the ridge and approached the structure, I saw it was more than a simple bamboo hut. It was made of wooden planks, rough cut but solid and squarely laid, with a thatch roof and front porch with as much floor space as the room inside. All of it was raised high off the land to keep snakes away and the floor dry when the rains came. The porch was enclosed by a low railing. Dtaw led me up the five short planks that were the steps so that I could stand and admire the view, its calming vastness.

"For you" he said, smiling.

"What?"

"This is for you." When I only looked at him in astonishment, he came closer, took my hands, and said, "I asked Cam to give us the land. When I came here last time, the neighbors helped me build it."

It was so like Dtaw to do something so generous and perfect, always without words.

"I love it," I said, knowing these words were inadequate for expressing how touched, how delighted, how amazed I was. But I didn't need to worry about the words. He could feel my happiness. I couldn't imagine someone giving away such a prime piece of land, but I knew enough of this culture to know that simply because I didn't understand something, that didn't mean it wasn't rational. And I also knew that with patience and attention, I might someday understand.

We spent the next few days reveling in our piece of paradise. We listened when the birds woke us before dawn, our baby between us, all of us lying on the thin grass mat, waiting to watch the first bright beams of sun cresting the horizon. Dtaw had built the cabin to face east. We made fires on the dirt to cook our simple meals of rice and dried meat. Over the fire we boiled the tea we drank while we sat in stillness as Cody slept or we attended to his needs. All of this added to the happiness I was already swimming in from the shock of maternal love that had become my life. I don't think I would have enjoyed mothering so much if I had expected to. Before having children, I had always thought babies, with their unattractive bodily functions and eating habits, were only just this side of gross and annoying. The idea that I could be so absorbed in the love of mothering was a double delight.

After a week in this new home, this retreat, we returned to the river, but now I knew we had this to come back to, an escape from the heat and mosquitoes and business of our life on the river. The quiet magic of the place stayed with me like a good secret.

ONE WORLD

*N*OW THAT WE WERE PARENTS, we realized we
needed to think more seriously about how to
support ourselves beyond the little we made
with the guest house and part-time teaching. At a friend's
suggestion, we decided to combine our love of bicycling
with our passion for learning about, respecting, and
preserving indigenous cultures. We created a bike tour
business we called One World Bicycle Expeditions. We
envisioned taking small groups of tourists beyond the
facade of Thailand's hotels and guest houses and into
"real" culture. Our mission was to support local indus-
tries while showing foreigners the elegance and beauty
of traditional ways of life. We were so familiar with the
Western and missionary perspectives on "developing"
countries as less advanced and in need of Western ideas
about education and progress. Our experience of local
culture was the opposite, that ancient beliefs and ways of
working with the land and communities were far more
sustainable and sensible than the capitalist model Western aid organizations espoused. We wanted to bring this
knowledge to foreigners. We also wanted to support or-

ganic farmers and villagers and craftspeople by bringing small groups of bikers through their communities in an environmentally low-impact way. It seemed to us that by increasing their markets we would be sharing the income we received from our clients and supporting rural economies. We had already seen the way the increased Westernization of Thailand was pulling able-bodied adults away from their villages to Bangkok and smaller cities in order to work in construction or kitchens or factories, to send money home to their families. This often meant young parents leaving their infants and children in the villages with grandparents. As young parents ourselves this seemed cruel, more to the parents than the children. We wanted to keep families together, and we thought the idea of bicycle expeditions might in some small way help with what we saw as a problem.

When Cody was six months old, we welcomed our first tour. We'd placed ads in *Bicycling* and *Adventure Cycling* magazines, and, much to my surprise, people had responded. This was in the early days of the Internet, so e-mail and websites were a novelty. I learned enough, though, to explain to potential clients that they'd have to mail me a check for the full amount of the tour *before* arriving in Thailand. Something must have made them trust us because they always did this without complaint. Dtaw and I imagined and created everything ourselves: the brochures we mailed to people, the routes, and the other logistics. Dtaw even designed a special removable rack for the van we rented to carry the bikes when we went to meet the clients at the airport in Udon, a city four hours away from our home. Cam agreed to ride with us to help on the tours. He took one of the new mountain bikes we'd purchased in Bangkok back with him to the village to practice using the gears and get used to riding long distances. He was a lifelong farmer and laborer, so strength and endurance wouldn't be a problem, but we needed to be sure he could be comfortable spending whole days on a bike.

We didn't think twice about whether or not to bring a six-month-old baby on the trips. Ever since returning to Thailand after Cody's birth, we had been taking him on long rides. With the upcoming tours in mind, we had arranged to have Burley, one of the first companies to make these lightweight contraptions for towing kids behind bikes, provide us one free of charge for the tours. We had brought Cody's car seat with us from America, and since he was too tiny to sit up and be strapped in with the trailer's safety belts, we cinched the car seat in and let him ride that way. We had to take numerous test rides before perfecting the shade we rigged with cloth and bungee cords to keep the hot sun off him during the long hours of riding. Once we had it right, we decided he was happy and comfortable riding along the river behind my bike. That first group of bikers was made up of Americans and a man from Israel who made himself Cody's honorary grandfather on the tour. Our clients seemed to enjoy having Cody's company along the way. We were so enamored of our son, we couldn't have imagined any other reaction.

The tour was a success. Everyone told us their eyes had been opened by the experiences they had meeting the hosts in the village homes where we slept on the floor and shared meals with the families. The clients loved stopping along the way to join farmers in the rice and cassava and cotton harvesting. They learned about weaving and dying and cooking and fermenting, all from standing beside the makers and taking part in the process. And, of course, the fresh organic meals we carefully planned to showcase the best, most wholesome local foods amazed people. We were far more satisfied than we'd ever imagined by seeing how Westerners' sense of "other" had been transformed by the trips. Together, Dtaw and I had created and executed a dream come true. Despite the challenges of running a business as a couple, we loved our new venture because we saw it as contributing to our shared vision of international understanding, a way to reinforce peace in a crazy world.

Trips were sporadic, so I continued to teach, and we continued to run our guest house, but the bike tours became our mission and passion.

~

BLESSING

~

*T*WO YEARS AFTER CODY AND JEW WERE BORN, I was pregnant again. My mother-in-law sat at the feet of the old monk in the temple at the end of our road as he listened to her words. His daily fast had been broken by the morning meal she and the other supplicants had cooked and brought from their homes. Mei Ya talked of the imminent birth of her eighth grandchild and asked for the blessing string that, properly blessed and tied, would keep the new baby safe and healthy. The monk turned to the spool of cotton string beside him and unwound a generous length of it, clipping it neatly with his teeth. Having been held in the hands of all twenty-one monks as they sat side by side reciting the holy scriptures and chanting over meals, this string was imbued with blessings.

The abbot turned back to Mei Ya and put a clean square of saffron-colored handkerchief on the smooth cement floor in front of where he sat on the platform above her kneeling figure. He lay the coil of string on the cloth so that he would not have to place it directly into her hands.

She raised her gnarled fingers, palms together, in

front of her forehead, the highest point of her body, to show the highest respect, reserved for monks and elders, and to thank him. She took the string without needing to think about touching his robes accidentally. She'd grown up with the knowledge that for a monk to have even his robes brushed by a woman was not permitted. That awareness was second nature for both. Settling back on her haunches, toes curled under her strong feet, she put her hands together high in front again, bent forward at the waist until her forehead kissed the cool cement, and pressed both palms flat against the floor. Immediately she rose back up to sitting, bringing her palms together again, and repeated the movement until she had bowed three times to honor each of the triple gems: the Buddha, the teachings, and the community of practitioners.

LABOR

*I*WANTED A HOME BIRTH, so we invited our midwife
Schyla, who had attended Cody's birth in Portland, to come to Thailand. Only half a generation
earlier, all births in this area had been home births, but
the miracle of Western medicine and the profitization of
health care had also brought the medicalization of birth.
By the time I was pregnant, home birth only existed in
the most remote villages.

Part of welcoming our American midwife included
trips into the outlying countryside to meet village mid-
wives and ask them about their experiences and opinions
of home birth. In one village, we stood in the yard next
to a bamboo hut talking with an old woman. She told us
about giving birth in the field as she worked. The wiry
woman squatted and put her hands below her crotch,
demonstrating the correct position for catching your own
baby. She reminded me, "Don't forget to tear the membranes with your fingers after it's born. Your new baby
will need to breathe, so you must remember to do this."
And there under the bright sky, she curved her forefinger
and middle finger into hooks and tore open the imaginary

bag around the imaginary baby between her legs.

I loved visiting these women, listening to them, letting them lay their hands on my huge belly to feel the baby's position and announce him perfectly ready to be born. I drank in the relaxed confidence with which they talked and moved. "It will be an easy birth." I heard this phrase repeated from each strong, wrinkled woman we met. I hoped so. An hour from any real medical care other than our midwife and the ill-equipped local hospital, I was counting on an easy birth.

The due date came and went. Schyla had been trying for weeks to help move me into labor with various tinctures and herbal teas. A few days after I started the Blue Cohosh, contractions like hard cramps began to twist around my belly. Each night I went to sleep sure I'd wake up ready to give birth. On the fifth day after the cramps had started, Schyla tried to stretch my cervix and strip the membranes. This should have caused cramps and backache, if not labor. Nothing.

The next step was castor oil. Schyla had heard of mixing it with cold Pepsi. Big mistake. Little clots of oil formed in the bubbles, and I could only manage one gulp before gagging. Putting it in the blender with grape juice and drinking it without even taking the time to put it in a glass made it possible to force most of the rest down. The gas it caused seemed to get things moving, with lots of cramps, but I woke up the next day still pregnant. On the tenth day, we talked about breaking the water, but when Schyla checked me, she found my cervix soft and thin and three centimeters dilated. She was able to stretch it out to six centimeters.

"It's got to be tonight," she said. "You're so open. Your cervix is like mush."

Three hours later I was in real labor, two weeks late and only a day before Schyla was scheduled to go back to Maine. By six p.m. the pains were five minutes apart. I sang to cope. "Puff the Magic Dragon," "All Glory, Laud and Honor." I needed enough of the lyrics to get me through one contraction at a time. Trying to keep the words and the tune gave me something to try to hold onto with my mind while the pain progressed. *"Life, I love you. All is groovy . . ."* As the intensity of the pain increased, I increased the volume of my singing to match it.

I kept searching for the best position to lessen the pain: on my knees, on my back, on my feet; but, of course, there was no position. The pain wasn't going away. I could feel part of each contraction in my back, some pressure, but not unbearable.

I told Schyla not to tell me how far apart the contractions were because I was afraid of engaging the logical, clock-watching part of my mind. I needed to be as unintellectual as possible for this, I knew. I needed to be my animal self. Finally, I settled on the back porch floor on my mat with three pillows.

As soon as I lay still and stopped trying to escape the pain, tried instead to fully experience it, things got easier. With every contraction, I reminded myself that it would end and even be short, not more than a minute or so. I visualized my cervix opening where the pain felt like a vertical slit midway between my pubic bone and belly button. My singing turned into wordless toning, louder and louder and higher and higher as the contraction built, dropping away as the pain did.

Schyla sat at my feet. Dtaw came back and forth from the kitchen with chicken broth, ice, apple juice, and popsicles. I was able to joke between contractions. Dtaw made me smile telling me about Cody's latest accomplishments: pouring juice, kicking a ball with his cousin.

I knew the neighbors could hear me, but no one complained about the singing cries that arose from our house every three minutes. I kept saying how this labor was so much easier than Cody's. It was good to be relaxed, not panicking, knowing my body would release this child. I enjoyed having Schyla's and Dtaw's full attention and support. I bossed them around without remorse.

"Schyla, move your toe off my mat. Dtaw, bring me a popsicle now. Don't hold my hand!"

Schyla assured me this was the perfect time to fully inhabit my goddess persona.

The pain intensified. I threw up twice. I remembered Schyla telling us in her birth class two years earlier that this was a great sign of opening and moving into transition.

Dtaw gave me his hand to hold, but when I did I felt as if I would slip out of the place of power I'd worked hard to maintain. I was afraid of falling into the role of victim to the pain, and when I held my husband's hand I started to feel like a weak, helpless woman, not a good attitude when facing the challenge of giving birth. I let go.

Schyla waited for a chance between contractions to put her fingers in my cervix to see how much progress I'd made.

"Katie, this baby is about to born," she almost shouted with excitement and relief. "You're nine centimeters dilated. I can feel his head and the water bag bulging out."

Dtaw and I looked at each other and laughed. I hadn't expected her to say that at all. Things just hadn't gotten that bad yet. After Cody's birth in the US when the Pitocin-induced labor ended up being a thirty-six-hour ordeal, I had expected much worse.

We had decided to have the birth in the bedroom, but there was momentary confusion as we considered doing it right there on the porch since I was so close. We finally settled on the bedroom and Schyla ran to unwrap her sterilized tools and prepare. While she was gone, Dtaw and I smiled at each other with anticipation.

In the dim plywood-walled room on the bed where this baby was conceived and where Dtaw had been born, I kneeled on all fours. Cody, Jew, Mei Ya, Cam, and Tong sat outside the open door, waiting, ready to welcome the newest member of the family.

"Okay, your water's going to break, and then you're going to have the baby," Schyla said before she rushed to the bathroom to wash her hands.

A contraction started to build. The bag exploded and water went everywhere.

"Schyla, Schyla!" Dtaw yelled. Dtaw is normally not a yeller.

"The water broke!" I shouted.

She returned and Dtaw hurried out to wash his hands.

"See," she said, pointing to the water all over the bed, "Totally clear." She was referring to Cody's birth, which had been complicated by meconium staining.

"What are those little bits of white stuff?" I asked.

"Vernix."

She suggested I lie back on the bed so she could massage my perineum to prepare it for the crowning. The massage sounded like a good idea, but changing my position seemed impossible.

Then another contraction started and I knew I had to try to push. I suddenly felt the baby's head pressing against my perineum.

"Ow! Ow! It hurts! It hurts!" I cried. This pain was much worse than the contractions. It was a sudden, raw, unfamiliar pain. I kept pushing to hurry up and get the baby out.

"Okay, do you want someone to call Cody and Jew so they can be here for the birth?" Schyla asked.

"I don't care. Just get this baby out," I gasped.

Then, all at once, I felt the joy of relief and looked behind me to see a little baby on his back on the wet bed, blue umbilical cord spiraling up from his belly button into me. He was crying. Dtaw picked him up. They wanted to give him to me.

"It's okay." I just wanted to catch my breath. I didn't need to hold him. His daddy had him. Then they started to pass him to me.

"The cord, the cord," I said.

They brought him back around and handed him to me through my legs. Somehow, I got up onto my knees and back onto the pillows.

We looked at the clock and marked the minute of the miracle. He had slid so perfectly into our world. I felt strong and proud and pleased. By now Cody, Jew, Mei Ya, Cam, and Tong were gathered around the bed.

"A perfect birth," Schyla announced.

Quiet and thoughtful, Chan lay on my breast in the yellow light of the hanging naked bulb. In no hurry to nurse, he seemed only interested in taking us all in. Silent, he watched as we admired him and murmured words of welcome. Schyla clamped the cord, not rushing to sever the physical tie between us.

Now everyone's attention was focused on my crotch, waiting for the placenta to tip out. I had no desire to push, but I could tell by looking at their faces how close it was to being out, though no one said a word until it fell onto the bed. Schyla scooped it into the big stainless steel bowl from the kitchen and examined it for integrity. She then asked if I was ready for Dtaw to cut the cord. I didn't care. Dtaw cut through the dense blue-and-white spiral with the sharp scissors.

Outside the crickets buzzed in the syrupy dark. Cody sat perched on the pillow by my right shoulder, nodding in and out of sleep. On my left, Jew sat with her small arm draped over my shoulders, smiling with a two-year-old's look of triumph for the first photos Cam was dutifully taking.

My mother-in-law came to me, looking from me to the baby. She'd been sitting for hours in the chair by the bedroom since she heard my labor cries before midnight. She had watched it all without concern, without interference. Birth was a simple fact in her world. She had borne six children, all at home, all with the help of only the village midwife.

In her hand, she held the blessing strings she'd been pulling back and forth between her fingers. While she waited, she'd tied a single overhand knot in the center of each one. She gently laid her hands on her grandson's tiny wrist and rolled the knot of it over his skin, back and forth, breathing words in Pali, the language of the Buddha, softly summoning blessings for health and wealth and happiness for this new child. She then joined the ends of the string on the other side of his wrists and tied the special knots she'd learned from her grandmother, knots that would keep all thirty-two spirits well-contained in his small body. If any of the spirits decided to go wandering, the consequences for the child could be disastrous.

After she'd seen to him, she turned her soft, wrinkled face to me, laid the next string across the back of my hand, repeated the blessing, and tied it off, rolling the knot against my inner wrist, rolling and blessing, rolling and blessing. I lay back to receive, too exhausted by the hours of labor and months of anticipation of this moment for anything other than being cared for.

Schyla called my mom back in Maine. Cam called the cousins down the street. Dtaw's sister called us. Schyla lifted Chan into the sling of her fish scale to weigh him: six pounds, eight ounces. Dtaw's mother hugged Schyla, and thanked her with tears in her eyes. Then all at once everyone was ready for bed.

How can they be tired? I thought. Things were just beginning. It was close to one a.m. Dtaw and Chan and I were alone together. Dtaw brought me a bowl of soup. I had a bath. We brought the baby into our clean bed, a thin mattress laid next to the open front doors to take advantage of the cool night breezes that wafted through. We lay and admired our new baby until just before dawn. He was four hours old when we all finally fell asleep.

After Chan's birth came the age-old tradition of the "mother fire" which would heal me and my baby. I lay on my bed of smooth strips of bamboo, sweat dripping down my shoulder and across my breasts. My belly slumped unevenly, no more the great round thing that it had been a few days before. Now only a lump of extra flesh as my uterus slowly contracted to its original size. The heat of the glowing coals in the fire close by soaked through my skin to my muscles and blood and bones, warming away the aches of a body stretched to its limits by the process of birth.

Over the mother fire an earthenware pot sat atop three stones set into the dried mud base of the low fire table Dtaw and Cody had built for me months before. Inside the pot, tea prepared specially for every new mother simmered: pink from the red sticks of wood Tong placed in the water early in the morning. The tree had been taken from the jungle by Cam with a prayer of thanks and dragged home and cut into pieces short enough for the pot. Then Tong and Mei Ya peeled off the bark and bundled stacks of the tea wood by the fire table for me and all the people who came to visit.

In those first days after Chan was born, I loved to lie with my belly close to the bamboo railing, built to support me, soaking in the fire's heat, watching the steam curl up and away from the handmade tea bowl. I loved to walk into the bathroom to find the aluminum basin filled with hot water for my bath, green from the herbs floating on the surface. I reminded myself each time of the effort Tong and Cam and my husband and mother-in-law had taken in carrying the heavy buckets of boiled water from the fire to the bathroom, four times each day, and in gathering the special leaves from farm and jungle. Every morning before I woke, Tong had started the fire, steamed the rice, started a fresh pot of tea, and heated a basin of bathwater over the fire. Quiet and strong and gentle, she was always there, smiling, soothing, supporting.

Everyone expected me to stay like that for three weeks at least. They were quite prepared to take care of me and Chan and not even allow me to get up. What a difference from the US. There, after the birth, you're sent home with no support. The parents are on their own. It's taken for granted that they will be utterly exhausted and miserable for the first month at least. In Thailand, in a tradition still followed in the more remote villages, after the birth, the mother is entirely cared for for two to four weeks. All the neighbors and friends and family help with holding and bathing the baby, washing diapers, sweeping, cooking. Aunts and cousins spend the night on mats on the floor to be with the new baby while the mother recovers.

My mother-in-law sorted and bundled the sticks for the tea, and with too much worry poured out three bowls at a time for me to drink, believing if I didn't drink enough I wouldn't have enough milk for Chan. Perhaps the right tea in copious amounts really was necessary to produce enough milk back when a woman followed tradition by eating only rice, galingale (a fragrant root like ginger), and salt for the first few weeks of her baby's life.

But as an outsider, I was able to pick and choose what traditions to follow, and in that more modern town, most women no longer followed such restrictive dietary practices as in the villages. Dtaw prepared special food for me each day. Black duck simmered in Chinese herbs, poached fish ordered specially from a market two hundred kilometers downriver, chicken steamed with lemon grass and shallots.

As Mei Ya held her new grandson that first day, she marveled at this tiny, incredible being, and crooned, "Now you see the sky. You're out here with us, and you finally get to see the sky." To me it sounded like she was saying to this newborn child, *We've been waiting for you. We've been wanting you, and now you're here with us. The world is huge and it's all yours.*

~~

KEEPING

~~

*T*HE DAY AFTER THE BIRTH, Dtaw came inside and called to Cody, *"Pai, Codte!"* (Come with me!) Two-year-old Cody jumped up from where he'd been playing with one of his plastic trucks to follow his daddy outside. I carried Chan over to the window and looked out to see the two of them at the back stairs, each with his own digging stick, a long handle made of a stout limb tipped with a rusty, rounded blade. Dtaw had made a small one, just right for Cody, and now, beside his father, he stood poking the dirt with it. They chatted like companions as they took turns stabbing their sticks into the deepening hole, levering up small heaps of rich brown soil. I loved this about Dtaw, the way he included Cody in his tasks in a way that allowed even a two-year-old to feel he was doing meaningful work with his father.

Dtaw and Cody leaned their sticks against the railing before they came inside. Soil sticking to Dtaw's sweaty face, he picked up a thick section of bamboo from the corner where he'd set it weeks before. Big around as his arm and two feet long, the bamboo was hollow but with a kind of floor at the bottom, like a giant test tube. In the jungle, these sections of bamboo, with stoppers of wadded-up leaves, served as water jug, cooking pot, or container. Tall thick stands of bamboo were so common in the jungle that a hunter usually didn't have far to walk to find a convenient container for whatever food he or she might need to carry home: fresh meat or grubs or ants.

Dtaw walked back to the kitchen, Cody following, and opened the refrigerator. From there he pulled out the plastic bag that held Chan's placenta. Carefully, he poured the placenta onto two sheets of thick handmade paper, rough and fibrous, bits of the *bai pu* tree it was made from still visible on the surface. Rolling the paper into a neat tube, he slid it into the section of bamboo Cody held up for him. Walking back through the house, they paused to smile and talk to Chan before heading down the steps, Cody chattering at his daddy as they walked. At the back steps, Dtaw leaned down and carefully set the bamboo section into the bottom of the hole. Together they pushed the soil over what had given Chan life while he was growing in my womb. Then, upending their sticks, they patted the dirt firmly into place with the round ends. This tradition of burying the placenta under the steps of the family home ensures that wherever a child goes, his spirit will always come home.

~~

BUSY

~~

I WAS MORE EXHAUSTED THAN I EXPECTED TO BE, mothering Jew and the boys in heat that brought on my asthma. But with Tong and Cam and the omnipresence of neighbors always happy to watch a toddler, things began to get easier. Every day my pleasure grew as I watched Dtaw parent our children. Watching him seemed to fill the hungry space I'd always had for a gentle, devoted father. He cooked for them, clowned with them, invited them to help him with his work in the garden and house. But what pleased me more than anything was seeing the way he was so clearly delighted by their presence. He held Chan especially close and spoke to him with quiet words.

Life finally felt good. I loved to watch Jew and Cody, now three years old, running in the street with their gang of friends chasing a ball or playing some complex game of tag. I loved standing at our gate at sunset when the shadows had lengthened enough to make being outside possible. Watching the children speed up and down while Tong held Chan, I stood at the ready with a bowl of rice soup filled with nutritious tender greens like the tiny ivy leaves I gathered from the garden. As one of the children raced by, I would lean down with a spoonful of good soup, saying, "Time to fill up with gas," and they would laugh, pretending to be race cars at the pump.

My favorite time of day was bedtime, when we all crowded in under the big mosquito net and the children shrieked with laughter while their daddy read an English picture book to them in his native Laotian, making up his own words and story. Even I, who had heard him tell the same stories dozens of times, could not help but smile as I watched their uncontrollable mirth and the way the four people I loved most in the world clutched each other in sheer love and joy as they fell off the pillow laughing. Then, finally, Jew's grandmother would come into the garden and call Jew home. I hated to give her up, but I knew that was the custom. She was a girl. She had to sleep with her grandmother, not her boy cousins. So we each hugged her goodbye until the early morning when she would come in through the garden gate and our day with her would start again.

When I became pregnant for the third time, we were delighted. Even so, I began to worry about our choice to live such simple lives. Knowing I would soon be a mother of three children, I started to think about our financial stability. Living as we did, we had little income. Teaching and running our guest house brought in only enough to buy food and the bare essentials. Leading bike trips, though it was a profitable business, always involved the risk that marketing costs would outweigh income. The trips were infrequent, and we could only make deposits into our small savings account when we happened to have clients.

I thought it was time to be more responsible. And I wanted my children to learn to read and write in English. We had been playing long enough, I thought, living the easy life of a half-US family in small-town Thailand where our days were spent biking, visiting farms, stopping to pick mangoes and papayas to slice open and eat right there. It was time to engage in what I imagined as "real" life for adults: jobs, savings accounts, education. And soon Jew would be going to live in Bangkok with her mother and father to start kindergarten.

With a new baby on the way, Dtaw and I talked often about what would be best for our children. We wanted them to live in a place where racism would not damage their sense of themselves as strong and smart and rich in cultural heritage. At the same time, I wanted the privilege I knew an American education would give them as adults. We could have sent them to an international school, but the idea of moving to a big city like Bangkok or Chiang Mai, where our schedules would be dictated by traffic patterns and where we would be far from trees and soil, didn't fit our vision for our family. Also, we worried, perhaps unfairly, that international schools served people who were in Thailand for work or profit, not people who were deeply connected to rural culture. Moving to the US would provide an American education while giving us what we hoped would be a more diverse community for them. Living in the US would be a huge change for all of us, but we were optimistic that we could be happy. I looked forward to giving birth where I knew it would be easy to find a home-birth midwife. I also looked forward to not struggling with asthma as I did in the tropical climate.

And I still missed my own culture. I had loved my elementary school teachers, and as Cody was nearing school age, I hoped he and Chan would have the same experience. We chose Seattle because we knew it had a robust Asian population and our Thai-American kids would not stand out as different. Its location on the northwest coast of the US made it feel close to Thailand.

~~

SEATTLE

~~

WHEN WE MOVED TO SEATTLE, we arrived in a city where we knew almost no one, with three duffle bags and $3,000 we'd saved from my salary teaching English and running the last bike tour. Coming from a Thai economy, that amount seemed like a fortune. We soon found how quickly life in America pulled money from our pockets. We wanted to live in a safe neighborhood with a good playground, so we could only afford a basement apartment. We shopped at garage sales and found a couple of futons and a coffee table, the extent of our furniture. We put the coffee table in the middle of the living room floor where we sat for meals. We didn't mind. In Thailand we always ate on the floor; that was the custom. We only needed the table to raise the food above the level of the shabby carpet. And who needed furniture with little boys? All the more room to run, we thought.

When the weather was nice, we'd carry our basket of sticky rice and whatever delicious dish Dtaw had cooked out onto the grassy strip between the apartment and the street, and eat there, enjoying the light and fresh air. It gave the boys a chance to run and play between the bites we'd pop into their mouths until the meal was done. We were always surprised that no one else was outside. How, we wondered, could so many people live in a city, yet we rarely saw any of them? So different from Thailand where we saw and heard our neighbors all day long.

We had to make money, so I started searching for a job. I was afraid no one would hire me because I was pregnant, so I looked for short-term employment. I taught summer school, worked as an on-call medical interpreter, and tutored. Whenever I came home from work, the boys would run and jump into my arms. The apartment was always fragrant with the smells of garlic and rice and curry or ginger from the meal Dtaw had ready for us. While we ate, the boys told me about their day, and we reveled in our good fortune of being a young family in love with one another.

Dtaw's first mission after finding an apartment was to procure bicycles for the boys. Chan was determined to be able to ride a two-wheeler by his third birthday, two months after the move. So Dtaw combed the springtime garage sales till he found bikes that were just right for both boys.

A few days before Chan's birthday, Cody and Dtaw took the training wheels off Chan's bike, and by the time he turned three, he'd mastered the skill of biking without them. As I watched Chan ride up and down the alley behind the apartment, he yelled, "Hey, Mom, look at this!" With that wonderful delight of a small boy first discovering his own skill, he lifted his little right hand high overhead and steered the bike along half the length of the alley with his left. When he whizzed past, bike wobbling slightly, his face shone with a smile just for me.

Only a week later he was saying, "Look, Mom, no hands!" And when we went to the park near our house, he and his brother rode down the long wheelchair ramps with the hairpin turns as easily as if they were flat wide roads. When they tired of that, they rode down the two dozen wide cement steps into the park.

People often commented on Chan's surprising agility and strength. It was clear even to strangers he had a special gift in the way he used his body. "You're too little to be on a bike without training wheels!" one woman's voice, friendly and amazed, called out as she slowed her car and craned her neck back to stare at the little boy on the red bike riding down the sidewalk in front of me in the sunshine. At a picnic a week earlier, Chan had been running around in the grassy park with only a shirt on, so that the muscles in his thighs were visible. A man nearby commented on what amazing grace and speed he had and how sure-footed he was for such a young boy. "How old is he?" he asked, with the same disbelief as the woman in the car.

"He turned three a month ago."

"Wow. That boy is going to grow into one fine athlete."

When Cody started kindergarten, Chan missed him every day. I bundled them both up in gloves and jackets to take the walk through the quiet neighborhood and down the hill to school. At the door, Cody and Chan kissed and hugged goodbye before Chan and I walked back home. As soon as we got home, Chan would ask the same question he would repeat throughout the day: "When do we pick up Cody?"

And I would answer, as I did every day, "After we go

to the playground and eat lunch and you have your nap."
Later, when we picked up Cody at school, Chan would
play with Cody and his friends in the schoolyard before
we all came home.

I asked Cody, after a few months of kindergarten,
when he'd had time to make some friends, if he ever
wanted to go play at their houses or have them over to
our place after school.

"No, I just want to come home and play with Chan,"
was his unvarying reply.

As my due date approached, it became clear that Dtaw
would have to work. His English was so limited that the
only jobs he could find were cooking in Thai restaurants.
It was hard work. Standing over the huge woks, stir-frying
hot chilies and steaming foods, burned his nasal passages,
already irritated from the allergies he'd developed from
the unfamiliar air of our new home. His arms and hands
would go numb at night from the repeated motion of his
job, and his bad back ached. Knowing the welfare of our
family would depend on him, he came up with a plan to
support us in a way that his minimum-wage job would
not.

He convinced me to accept one of the offers from
the credit card companies to take out a loan. I had never
done so, and the idea scared me, but I put my faith in his
abilities and filled out the short application. Soon we had
$5,000 to invest in Dtaw's business idea: selling Thai food
at festivals around the state. We bought a beat-up yellow
van, tore out the seats, and filled it every weekend with
the heavy equipment Dtaw had picked out from the huge
restaurant supply store downtown—steam table, portable

gas burner, enormous wok, a tent with sandbags to weigh it down when the wind came. It got so full that there was nowhere to sit, so the boys and I followed behind in our little blue Toyota every weekend morning at four a.m. as Dtaw led us out of the city and around the state of Washington to sell food.

During the week Dtaw experimented with recipes for Thai iced tea, the perfect pad thai sauce, and marinade for the satay. These he prepared in huge pots. He often stayed up all night cooking and stirring before a festival. During the week he threaded carefully cut chunks of raw chicken breast onto endless skewers of bamboo that packed the freezer. He was sleep-deprived, his back ached, but he was determined to succeed. We did well at the festivals. The food was amazing and soon people were lining up. The boys helped at the busy times, running back and forth between me at the cash drawer and their daddy at the stove, conveying orders and grabbing plastic forks or bags or food as instructed. The work was exhausting, but we were doing it together, and by the end of the summer we were able to pay back the loan.

"But Mama, why can't I go with Cody to the birthday party?" Chan looked up at me, his brow furrowed. Never in the nearly four years of his life had he been excluded from an experience that his brother was part of. In Thailand children played together as a pack. No one was ever singled out for something special like a party. Whenever Dtaw started up the rumbling engine of our 1966 Land Rover, Cody and Chan and their cousins and neighbor children came running, climbing and tumbling into the benches in the back, ready for adventure.

"Things are different in America. Little brothers are not invited to birthday parties, I guess."

"Maybe you could call and see if they made a mistake," Chan suggested.

"Okay, I will, sweetie."

There was no mistake. It was a birthday party for five-year-olds. No, they gently replied, they couldn't make an exception for Chan. Three was too little.

This would be Cody's first birthday party. In Thailand birthdays were celebrated quietly by a morning visit to the temple with offerings for the monks. No gifts, no cake, no parties. People who celebrated the day of their birth (and many did not) did so with the much-practiced act of giving rather than receiving.

The day of the party I buckled Cody and Chan into their car seats and carefully followed the directions Cody's friend's dad had given us over the phone. When we pulled up to the house, I let Chan walk Cody to the door, hoping the parents would see the absurdity of their choice, see what a well-behaved and charming child he was, standing hand in hand with Cody, then relent and invite him in. But despite having been born and raised in this culture, I underestimated the strength of its social norms. I had lived in Thailand for the better part of a decade. I had done all my mothering there, so now my own American ways seemed almost foreign to me.

Chan came walking back down the steps alone, a little slower than usual, a mix of resignation and bewilderment on his face.

"Oh, honey, I'm sorry they didn't let you come in."

He sat silent in his seat as we drove away, leaving his brother behind.

* * *

Luckily for Chan, I was six months pregnant when Cody started school. Each time the baby began to move inside me, I called to Chan, "Hurry, Baby's moving!" and Chan would jump up from his blocks or train set and come running across the living room to put his small hands under my shirt, waiting to feel the next movement. Then his face would shine with wonder as he looked up, wide-eyed, at his miracle-making mama.

As the due date approached, I noticed that Baby was especially active when I took a bath, so at night while Dtaw cooked beef curry with coconut milk or chicken soup with galingale or pork fried with pepper and garlic or any other of his delectable meals, the boys and I would crowd into the tub of our small, subterranean apartment and wait. With their hands on my belly, and the warm water quieting around us, we watched and felt the coming life in the strange movements tunneling across my flesh or the bump rising and falling almost before we saw it.

"Cody! Cody! Did you see that?" Chan would call out.

"Yeah," Cody would shout back, his ragged voice echoing off the walls of the tiny bathroom, "keep looking! Baby's gonna move again!"

From the moment Baby was finally born, at home in our bed, Chan wanted to be by his side. When friends came to visit, Chan would reach up to where I held the new baby in my arms and, tenderly touching his brother's feet, say, "Look! Look how tiny his toes are!" smiling as proud as if he had fashioned them himself. "I love his toes!"

At Baby's first checkup, Chan accompanied us into the examining room saying, "Don't worry, Baby. Dr. Ben is really nice. You will like him." The young doctor came in and chatted with Chan about his new brother. Then, pulling up Baby's shirt, Dr. Ben said, "Let's have a look at that stump. I want to see how it's healing."

"It's called an umbilicus," came Chan's small voice, clear and firm, from where he stood, fingers resting on the edge of the examining table.

Dr. Ben smiled, looked at me, then back down at Chan. "You are right. I'm sorry. I'll try to use the correct terminology from now on."

It was two weeks before we settled on a name for the new baby.

"I think you should name him Chan," Chan told me.

"But honey, that's your name."

"I know. I still think his name should be Chan."

This conversation was repeated several times each day. We settled on Tahn. In Thai it means water or stream. Because the Mekong River was so significant to Dtaw and me, having fallen in love at its side and biked into Tibet, following its course as much as we could, it seemed a good name. And I hoped because the sound of the name was so close to his, Chan would be satisfied.

Chan, in Pali, means enlightenment or calm awareness. It is also the Chinese word for Zen. Zen was the name we gave the first thing Dtaw and I made together, the guest house for foreign backpackers in Dtaw's hometown.

Cody's name came from *codte*, an archaic Laotian word for roots of a tree or roots of the family, ancestors. When Dtaw explained the meaning of his first-born's name to friends in Thailand, they invariably laughed, not out of disrespect, but more from admiration tinged with fear. They grew up with Thai as the dominant power language. The language of their homes and families, Laotian was to be hidden, forgotten in the quest for education, betterment, progress, Westernization. But Dtaw never believed in all that. He always held a deep respect for the elders in his family and community. And he honored their history as indigenous people.

HOME

DTAW'S SISTER JUM AND SIX-YEAR-OLD JEW
stood waiting at the front of the crowd in the
Bangkok Airport. Taller and thinner, dark hair
longer, Jew beamed at us and then her mother when she
saw us. Jum looked more tired than before. The boys began to run when they spotted their cousins and aunt, respectful *wai*'s first, then hugs all around. Jew laughed at
seeing Cody's long hair and new clothes. Each of us held
the hand of someone we hadn't seen for too long as we
made our way to Jum's little car. Squeezed into the front
with Tahn on my lap, I turned to watch Cody laughing
with Jew, the smile I had almost forgotten shining again
on his face.

In Seattle, the strain of raising young children without extended family, working to pay rent, and getting
food on the table had taken such a toll on Dtaw and me
that a year after Tahn's birth, we had decided to return
home to Thailand. Stress had become a part of Cody's
daily fare too, hurrying to school, being wary of strangers, watching over his brother—it was as if a shell had begun to cover Cody's light. And now I watched it crumble

away in that first moment of contact with Jew, his cousin, his almost twin. I could have cried with relief and pleasure. Until that moment, I hadn't realized how hard Cody had worked to be American.

We traveled on the overnight bus the next evening to our house on the river. Back at home on our little street, the boys fell right back into playing with all the zest they'd always had. Cody quickly became the leader of his small pack and there was always a spot for Chan at his side. Still quiet, but funny and sly and always ready to make a joke, Chan was a typical middle child, a settling presence for all of us. The two older brothers and Jew doted on Baby Tahn with as much devotion as they'd received as infants. I finally began to feel a sense that things were right, that I could release the tension I'd gathered living in the US. I had the distinct sense that I could stop worrying that some disaster was about to unfold, that I could relax and simply enjoy the goodness of family life without worrying about paying rent or finding work or being isolated in a small apartment in the suburbs. At last things felt as if we were finally where we belonged.

Between organizing bicycle tours and tutoring English, there was plenty of time for biking and playing soccer, for taking drives to visit friends, for walks along the river. Dtaw and I had bought a second bike trailer in Seattle, so now the five of us could take rides through the rice fields and hills around our village. Jew and Cody giggled and talked together in one trailer behind Dtaw's bike, while from his trailer behind mine, Chan clowned with Tahn in the plastic seat on my rear rack.

Whatever the combination, we all loved our early-morning rides through the countryside where Dtaw would stop in the middle of a village when he saw something that he knew would interest the children and me—an old couple shredding tobacco leaves, a blacksmith and his apprentices forging steel into sharp blades for the upcoming rice harvest, or a family loading wood into a hollow mound of dry mud, their kiln for transforming trees into charcoal.

Whenever he stopped, we always knew we were about to meet some interesting people and learn something about the traditions of his culture. The boys and Jew would climb out, sometimes sleepy from dozing. I would lift Tahn from his seat, and the residents of the farm where we had stopped, whether friends, cousins, or strangers, would immediately lead the children off to the shade for cool water or chunks of fresh papaya or coconut they'd pull from a tree.

Dtaw began the conversations in no hurry to learn anything in particular, with plenty of room for silences to listen to the breezes rustling the palm fronds. He would ask the old man or woman he was talking to about their farm and children and hometown. Inevitably, though never in any hurry, the person would ask Dtaw about his family and would discover that Dtaw was the son of Gla the tailor. Whether the man was a stranger, old friend, longtime customer, or a distant cousin, there were always exclamations of admiration and warmth at hearing that Gla's son and his family were among them. When the realization came of who Dtaw's father was, we would be embraced with even greater welcome and pleasure.

I felt at these moments that there was no question about the reality of karma carrying past us into the future.

Gla's easygoing manner put people at ease. Half a century after his good works, his integrity and kindness still ensured a warm welcome for his grandchildren throughout the province. Eventually Dtaw would ask the host about the work at hand. We were able to touch or taste or try whatever we were seeing. Any concerns I might have had about taking Cody out of school to come home to Thailand vanished on these outings.

PART 2

LEARNING

I N MAY OF 2002, Cody and Chan joined their friends and neighbors in starting school. Chan was delighted with his custom-made uniform, his name neatly embroidered in Thai lettering in blue thread over his left chest pocket. I took a job teaching English at a school a few miles down the road from their schools so I could drop them off on my way to work and we could ride home together each day on the city bus. On the long ride, I would lean back in my seat, exhausted, while the boys giggled from behind me as they pretended to "wash" my hair for me; their motive: messing up my teacherly look. I didn't care about my hair. The sound of their happiness in one another was all I needed.

Chan attended the lab school at the teacher's college in the provincial capital. The bus dropped us off on the side of a highway teeming with speeding cars and *song teows*, converted pickup trucks with long benches where students crowded and hung off the back, holding the bars as the vehicles careened around corners. In front of the college, an overpass for pedestrians spanned the highway, and each morning Chan and I climbed the long cement staircase to the top, then walked high above the traffic to the other side. In the distance back toward home, blue mountains melted into morning mist. At the end of the bridge, we climbed down and walked a couple hundred yards along the shoulder and up the drive of the shady campus to the entrance of his school.

After a few weeks, Chan, not quite five, insisted he didn't need to be walked to school. He could get off the bus and walk over the highway and into the campus alone. I resisted. He was still so young. The cars were so dangerous. He persisted. He also knew that after I left him, I then had to go back across the highway to wait for a song teow to carry me the last miles to my school. Maybe he wanted to save me the trouble. After several mealtime discussions that involved the whole family, he agreed that I would get off the bus with him and walk him halfway over the bridge, and from there he'd walk to school alone.

The day arrived to carry out our plan. When he let go of my hand in the middle of the bridge and turned his face up for a hug and a kiss, I held him a long time. Pulling away, he looked at me intently, "Don't *worry*, Mom. I'll be *fine*," he said with a firm tone. I watched his small figure, new backpack bobbing behind him, as he walked away and disappeared down the steps. Once he was safely inside the low walls of the campus, I hurried to the far end of the bridge so I could get a clear view of him heading up the driveway, hoping he wouldn't glance back to see me cheating on our agreement. He walked steadily away, not looking back, and I felt the tears slide down my cheeks as I, too, turned and walked into my day.

Six weeks later, in July, I was working to harness the wild

momentum of a hot roomful of energetic students in their bright white uniforms, trimmed in navy blue, nearly fifty of them rearranging themselves for another raucous game of English Occupations. I was concentrating every bit of my teaching mind on containing their enthusiasm and mischief before it turned to chaos.

Five minutes before the end of class, something made me turn my head toward the door, where I was surprised and delighted to see Chan standing hand-in-hand with his father. He smiled happily, if a little shyly, at his loud, busy teaching mother. A rush of some brain chemical suspended the clatter of the chairs and chattering students the moment I saw him, my funny, sweet middle child.

I'd forgotten they were coming into town that day for what we thought was an unremarkable doctor's visit. Chan, normally healthy, had been exhibiting strange symptoms since the tetanus shot he'd had in December. First a cold with sores on his throat that took weeks to heal, then a pimple on his nose, odd for a four-year-old. And recently he'd been throwing up just a little bit before school each day. I waved it all off as new-student jitters, but when a small sty appeared on his eyelid, Dtaw insisted he see a doctor.

I motioned to Dtaw that they should wait a few minutes on the bench outside the classroom while I finished up with my students. As I turned my attention back to the class, a newly familiar sense of warmth and gratitude spread through me. Recently this strange sense of calm had been coming to me. My life seemed to have settled down. After the stress of living in the US, I was beginning to relax. I was noticing for the first time in my life that I was surrounded by people I loved and who loved me. Even my cheeky students with their dirty fingernails and loud, ungrammatical English brought out a sense of motherly love whenever I saw them.

I hurried to finish the lesson, so I would have time to introduce my son to my students. But when I stepped outside to invite Chan and his father into the room, they had disappeared.

"Chan! Dtaw!" I called out. When no answer came, I hurried down the smooth wide hall searching for them. They were neither on the landing nor the stairs, nor resting in a vacant chalk-dusty classroom.

For no reason I could imagine, I felt an alarming sense of dismay. I rushed back and dismissed my class, gathered up my papers, and, in a daze, hurried to an empty classroom. I shut the door and let my sobs escape with a vehemence that surprised me. It wasn't like me to fall apart in the middle of a workday. *I'll see him after school*, I told myself. *It's not as if he's gone forever.* I cried as if my heart had suddenly broken, though I couldn't imagine why, then dried my eyes for my next class.

That day the doctor ordered a blood test for anemia. The results provided a diagnosis of thalassemia, a common condition in northeast Thailand, and we were told to give Chan iron pills and to prepare for the possibility that he might not be able to play sports in high school or have children. I needed to know more, so over the course of the next few weeks, I visited several doctors, learning to match their patronizing brush-offs with patient but stubborn insistence. Finally I found one who told me it could be aplastic anemia, leukemia, or thalassemia, and that Chan should be seen by a specialist in another city. All those words sounded alike to me, but leukemia was more familiar. "What's leukemia?" I asked.

"Bone marrow cancer."

Eight of us—the boys, Jew, Dtaw, Mei Ya, Jum, and I—arrived at the university hospital in Khon Khaen, a four-hour drive from home. After hours in the waiting room, crowded with whole families, we were finally seen by a doctor. She explained that Chan would be checked in and later given a bone marrow aspirate. It was late afternoon before the surgeon sent for us. Most of the family went to a cousin's house to spend the night. Dtaw, Chan, and I moved into his room.

In our hospital room, empty except for the small table and bed, iron bars half-coated in chipped white paint, the surgeon addressed Chan: "You're going to have to hold very still, do you think you can do that?"

Chan nodded, face solemn, matching the doctor's expression.

"It's going to hurt, but not for long. I'm going to insert a long needle into your hip bone and draw out some marrow so we can look at it," the doctor continued. "Your mother and father will be right here with you, so you can hold their hands if you want, but it's very important that you not move before I take the needle out."

Chan nodded again. I was grateful that the doctor addressed Chan as he would an adult. That is one of the things I appreciated about raising my sons in Thailand. People expected children to be able to handle life and the pain and suffering that goes with it. They didn't expect them to do it without ever crying and complaining, but there was no sugar-coating of the fact that life includes hardship.

"You can cry and scream all you want to when we're finished, but not during the procedure. Okay?" the doctor reiterated.

"Okay," Chan answered.

It was normal practice in Thailand to avoid general anesthesia whenever possible, even with children. I believed that anesthesia hid the pain, rather than stopped it. I was aware that anesthesia is normally administered along with what is known in the trade as "milk of amnesia," a drug that induces a state of forgetfulness about the experience, so that the patient cannot consciously remember it. To me that meant it also made total healing from the experience impossible. Without the ability to access the memory of the pain, how could one later release it?

A little later, the doctor came back to the room to take us across the hall to an examining room with bare floors, cement walls, and a steel examining table bolted to the floor. I lifted Chan up onto the high table. The doctor asked him to pull his pants down over his bottom and lie on his belly. He did so.

Dtaw and I stood close by, smiling our reassurance and faith in Chan. Inside I trembled. The doctor spoke casually to Chan as he unwrapped the needle he held below the table, out of Chan's sight. When he told Chan to look at us and keep very still, raising the needle over Chan's hip, I could see why. The needle itself was six inches long and an eighth of an inch in diameter. I summoned all my mothering skills to keep the alarm from showing in my face. Focusing intently on the insertion spot in Chan's hip, the doctor slipped the point into the soft flesh. Chan grimaced, but held still. Dtaw and I held our breath, watching the doctor draw back the plunger and the syringe slowly fill with a golden bubbling liquid. Chan didn't move. At last the marrow had filled the tube and the doctor pulled out the needle and stepped back. We all exhaled. Chan pulled up his pants and stood up to come into my arms, his mouth set in a thin line.

Once we were back in our room, and the nurses had left us, Chan started to cry. I told him I understood it must have hurt tremendously and he had been so brave. It was good to cry now, I kept telling him, as he let the painful experience shudder out of him in my embrace.

Later that night, while we looked down at the city lights, a curiosity for all of us, accustomed to the darkness of our garden at night, Chan spoke up: "I think there must be a lot of good toy stores out there, Paw. I think tomorrow you should go get me a really cool new toy like you promised."

"Of course I will," his daddy replied. As we lay side by side, the three of us in the single bed with iron rails, Dtaw talked about how brave Chan had been and said that when we woke up in the morning, he'd go right out to get him that special toy he'd promised. I worried that Chan could see our fears spelled out in our eagerness to buy him a reward for doing something hard. He would know that wasn't like us. But I couldn't think what else to do.

We lay together cuddling Chan between us while Dtaw spoke to him in the soothing voice that always helped the children and me sleep. Finally, Chan's breathing slowed and steadied, and the two of us dozed in the dark. At around nine o'clock that night, a knock sounded on the door. A nurse stepped in. "The doctor would like to talk to you."

Dtaw and I exchanged looks. The doctor who took Chan's marrow that morning had told us that another doctor would look at the cells under a microscope and give us the diagnosis later that day. We knew we were about to hear what might be wrong with Chan's blood. *Aplastic anemia, leukemia, thalassemia.* These words tumbled in my head like poetry.

We followed the nurse into the unlit hallway that served as a long balcony so that we could feel the night breeze on our skin and hear the hum of crickets in the grass below. Immediately outside the door, a doctor stood with a knot of a dozen young medical students in white coats. The doctor looked at us, yellow light spilling from the room and illuminating the side of his face. He spoke to us without acknowledging the students gathered in close, listening.

"I have examined your son's marrow," he began, "and it is clear to me that he has acute myeloid leukemia, bone marrow cancer. I think it is of the M6 variety, but that is difficult to diagnose only with the naked eye and a microscope. You will need to travel immediately to Seattle, Washington, for cytogenetic testing and diagnosis. They have more advanced technology there." As he spoke, my legs felt weak and I looked around at the curious students. I wondered why they were there. I wondered why no one was asking me if I needed to sit down. I wanted to ask someone to bring me a chair, but as so often happened when I lived in that culture that was not my own, I suppressed my own needs in order to follow what seemed appropriate. I concentrated on staying vertical as I tried to make sense of the doctor's words. A product of my racist culture, I thought, *Oh no. I never should have married a Thai man. This must be the result of trying to mix incompatible genes.* Already I had begun the incessant worry that this was somehow my fault.

The doctor seemed to read my mind. "This is entirely a fluke. It has nothing to do with your genes as parents. There is less than a one-in–one hundred million chance that this kind of genetic abnormality would express itself. Medicine does not know why it happened. There is no explanation. Do not try to find one. Do not try to look for a cause. You will not find an answer."

As he spoke, I closed my eyes and saw black-and-white images of genes and mitochondria that swam up from seventh grade studies of biology. I saw the cell diagrams I had so painstakingly drawn, but in my mind they swirled like mutated fingerprints. I took deep breaths.

"You will need to travel immediately to the Hutchinson Center in Seattle where the first bone marrow transplant was conducted to begin treatment with aggressive chemotherapy." I couldn't believe this was real.

The doctor and students moved on. Dtaw and I were left to sit limp on the edge of the bed where Chan slept. Dazed, slammed, we sat in silence. We lay down and held each other close.

"It's going to be okay," Dtaw murmured into the top of my head. "We will figure this out. Chan is very strong. We will fight."

"But how?"

We stayed up talking about the options, Western allopathic vs. Eastern holistic medicine. He had heard of a nutritionist in Bangkok who specialized in helping people overcome cancer without allopathic treatment and chemotherapy. We had heard many stories of people healing from diseases using the powers of jungle plants, spirit doctors, and meditation. We went back and forth over the possibilities.

"Honey," I said at last, "this is cancer. As much as I believe in homeopathy for taking care of colds and fevers the boys have gotten, and as much as I am averse to allopathic medicine and want to believe in traditional Thai treatments, I don't think we can decide what to do based on what makes me comfortable. We need to do what will make Chan well, whether it matches up to my antiestablishment politics or not."

Dtaw was quiet, then nodded, and we agreed that we would listen to the doctors and return to Seattle.

As Dtaw drove us home that night, I held Chan close in my lap and looked out at the fiery orange and solemn gray skies shining in the flooded rice fields and wept silently. I was so afraid we would whisk him off to the US for treatment and he would die there, afraid he would never be able to come back to his beautiful homeland.

A week later Chan and I were headed to his first appointment at Seattle Children's Hospital. Dtaw and Cody stayed behind with Tahn to pack up and move our family back across the Pacific two weeks later.

PART 3

~~~

TREATMENT

~~~

W ITHIN SEVENTY-TWO HOURS of a second bone marrow aspirate and confirmation of the diagnosis the doctor in Thailand had made, Chan was checked into a sunny room on the cancer ward at Seattle Children's Hospital. With a huge picture window on one side of the room and a glass wall between his bed and the center of the ward on the other, there was plenty to see. We watched as nurses and patients and families walked by. It almost felt homey, the way people came and went like neighbors. Nurses bustled in and out, friendly, welcoming. Social workers were sent to guide me through the dizzying challenge of insurance forms and medical histories. They knew that the news of a child's cancer diagnosis would make the processes of bureaucracy impossible without gentle persistent help. Systems were in place for this. All I had to do was what they told me.

There had been another kind of worry for a few days before Chan's aspirate. The oncologist met with us to tell us that it was not clear that Washington State Medicaid would cover Chan's hospital bills because we had been living overseas. She told us that Chan's medical costs could amount to well over half a million dollars. Despite the enormity of this number and having no savings at the time, we didn't think much about it. A lifetime of debt sounded at that point like the least of our worries. It was still a relief, though, when she told us the next day that even if the state wouldn't cover the bills, the hospital would find the funds to make sure Chan received the care he needed. After Chan was admitted, we were informed that Medicaid would pay for his care after all.

Before the chemo started, Chan would need a Hickman line surgically inserted just above his heart. This was done so the toxic chemo drugs could be conducted into his body without exhausting his forearm veins. One of the nurses explained that only one adult would be able to stay in the room at night. The rest of the family could come during daytime visiting hours. The five of us had always slept close together. We contested the policy, but we did not win.

A few days after the first doses of chemo had been pushed into the line, one of our nurses took me aside to give me some advice: "When his hair starts falling out, it's going to be itchy and messy. And it won't look good. You might want to consider shaving his head before that happens. We have clippers. I'd be happy to do it for him."

Grateful for her wisdom, I consulted Dtaw. Because he was always skilled at getting the children to do what he wanted them to, I left it to him to bring it up with Chan.

"Mama!" Chan, excited and happy, called to me as soon as I'd opened the door to step into the room the next morning. "Guess what? I am going to have my head shaved."

As soon as the last clump of soft brown hair fell to the floor, Chan grabbed up his bedsheet and wrapped it around his waist and over one shoulder, monk style. "Look, Mama! I'm a monk!" He picked up the clean plastic basin by his bed for the nausea that would hit hard in the night and held it like an alms bowl as he pretended to make the morning rounds.

I pulled the movie *The Black Stallion* off the shelf from the line of videos in their worn cardboard cases. I remembered liking the movie when I was young, so I took it back to the room and offered it to Chan. During his stays in the hospital, the threat of infection was taken seriously because of his suppressed immune system. He was never allowed to leave the floor and was discouraged from leaving his room. Other children were not allowed to visit, and even his brothers' visiting hours were limited. After raising my boys without television or Internet in our home, and after realizing how much physical pain would be involved in chemo medications, I quickly succumbed to our rapturous forays into the world of television. *Dora the Explorer, Johnny Bravo,* and *Kim Possible* became companions I could depend on being cheerful and strong.

I also allowed a movie every couple of days. I had been a mother who eschewed antibiotics and food grown with pesticides. In Thailand we had so much fresh air and sunshine that even indoors we were outdoors. Our traditional house had no glass in the many windows and the breezes and the neighbors moved freely in and out. We had shaped our lives not around career and financial planning but around a healthy lifestyle.

Yet here we were, in urban America to treat our middle son for bone marrow cancer. With the onset of his disease, I quickly began to relinquish the tight grip I had held on my ideas of how to grow healthy children. Television became one of the earliest concessions, right after Western medicine.

Chan watched the movie rapt. In it, an aged Mickey Rooney helps a bereaved boy and his horse to overcome their life-threatening obstacles and achieve greatness together. Chan told everyone about it. "Have you seen *The Black Scallion?*" he would ask his favorite nurses. I never corrected his mispronunciation. He would go on to tell with wide-eyed enthusiasm the struggle of the young boy and the way the horse saved him.

Days later, and for the months of treatment that followed, when the diarrhea and vomiting and itching became so bad that Chan wept, Dtaw soothed him by telling him that when we returned home to Thailand, he would buy him his own black stallion.

~~~

TRADE

~~~

FOR THE NEXT SIX MONTHS, we lived in an apartment in the University of Washington's graduate student housing a mile and a half from the hospital. We were lucky to find this apartment, a modern place just right for us. Clean and new, furnished simply, it was part of a spacious complex of student housing with other young international families nearby. One of the three playgrounds built into the sloping lawns was twenty feet from our back door. With three boys under six, this was a godsend.

Work was out of the question. Both Dtaw and I were overtaxed for time and energy with all the responsibilities of caring for the boys and Chan. My generous mother paid the rent on the apartment and whatever else we needed. We didn't need much. Insurance would cover all Chan's medical bills, and as we had lived in Seattle before, we had a whole community of friends and acquaintances and even people we'd never met who organized themselves into a support system for us. They divided up the chores of grocery shopping, cooking dinners, and shuttling Cody to and from the small school where he was in first grade.

They even took care of Tahn so that Dtaw and I could focus on getting Chan everything he needed. They did all of this without troubling us for input. I only knew that when we came home at night from the hospital, groceries were in the fridge and dinner was waiting in containers on the counter. A friend even gave us her old minivan so we could get back and forth to the hospital each day.

Seattle Children's Hospital became our second home. We juggled cooking for Chan, soothing his chemo reactions, parenting the other two, and holding as tightly as we could to our sanity. For me, this required suppressing all my fears to be able to keep up with the constant physical demands of caring for a very sick child. Chan underwent two four-week rounds of inpatient intensive chemotherapy. He emerged seeming very much intact despite the painful side effects throughout.

Four months after treatment had begun, it looked as if Chan was on the road to recovery. The percentage of young cells in his body seemed to be returning to normal and his energy was high. He was finally home with us, making us all grin with delight as we watched him run and play with his brothers.

We could have stopped there, walked away from the table without looking for higher returns. We could have hoped that the chemo alone would be enough to cure him, that his body would return itself to balance. We might have, but Chan's doctors told us that cytogenetic testing showed that his DNA still carried a tiny abnormality on one of the chromosomes. Because of this, they suggested he have a bone marrow transplant to replace his own marrow with that of a healthy donor. There were so few people who had ever been diagnosed with this particular kind of leukemia that no reliable statistics could be studied. They could not project the outcome of waiting to see how the effects of the chemo would pan out. They did say that if we wanted to go with a transplant, it should be done quickly, while the cancer was still at bay from the chemo. The only odds they could give us on this gamble were that the transplant itself had as much a chance of killing him as it did of saving him.

~~~

CONDITIONING

~~~

W E FOLLOWED THE DOCTORS' ADVICE and took him in for what they called "conditioning," toxic radiation that would kill his own cancer-producing marrow to replace it with marrow we hoped would produce healthy cells.

In the basement of one of the University of Washington's largest buildings, a bank of fluorescent lights glared down from the ceiling illuminating pale yellow walls and an expanse of white linoleum floor in this cavernous room that would soon swallow my child. I wondered how such a tall space could exist underground. It had taken some time for Chan and me to wind through the warren of hallways before we found the office where a nurse led us downstairs to the world of busy researchers, students, doctors, and a few frightened-looking patients.

The radiation room waited, empty except for the steel table in the middle with the linear accelerator poised above it like a mechanical claw. This, they explained to me, was where my son would lie, unconscious, while his marrow—the marrow that had grown inside my body inside him—would be altered, damaged beyond repair. I stood looking at the setup and tried to understand this protocol.

The room was cold. I knew he would be naked with his eyes taped shut so as not to fall open and disturb the technicians as they worked. The cast that had been molded to stop the radiation from entering his chest and ruining his lungs would rest upon his slender body. I knew they would do their work, adjusting angles, straightening his head, picking up and carefully settling his limbs on the chill of the table, perhaps warmed a bit by the insistent heat of his body, and I knew I would not be there to protect him.

The doctor was adamant. No, he could not go through radiation and be conscious. I pleaded, explaining how mature he was, how good he was at holding still in uncomfortable places, but the doctor refused. And no, I could not stay in the room, not sit very quietly behind the technicians at the control desk, not bothering anyone.

No, I could not even stand at the window outside, alone, peering in at my son. There was nothing they would let me do to keep him safe, to keep watch.

So when the time came, he and I both smiled bravely just before they settled the anesthesia mask over his face and ushered me out.

The waiting room was small and dark with a ceiling low enough that it seemed to press down on me. I sat in an easy chair with fabric so acrylic I shrank from its touch. A nurse had been assigned to sit with me, to keep me company. But I would have felt better alone, easier to sink into the fear and doubt that saturated my mind. What had I done? Listened to the doctors offering up my child's body as a sacrifice to their gods of medical technology I had always had so little faith in? Even the doctors were not sure. The head oncologist's words reverberated in my head. *The transplant could kill him . . . Fifty-fifty chance that the bone marrow transplant itself will end his life.* Why had we chosen this route? Up until that morning, we could have changed our minds, turned back, back to nature, to his own resilience. But not now. The radiation would kill him if the doctors didn't swoop in and save him with their miracle of a stranger's marrow.

I was there by myself. Dtaw had to take Cody to school and drop Tahn off with another generous friend who'd agreed to watch him. By the time Chan came out of the anesthesia hours later, though, we were all gathered around him, his brothers laughing at his sleepy face. They asked him what it was like. He roused himself quickly at the sound of his brothers' voices and talked with his usual enthusiasm, delighted in the novelty of a new treatment center, nice nurses, and all the apple juice he wanted.

Except for the misery of chemotherapy's physical effects, Chan enjoyed the adventure of the hospitals where he was the center of attention and there was always something new to see. Adults were keenly interested in his health and what he had to say. Doctors listened intently to not only his heart and lungs, but to his words. Even the frequent blood draws were interesting to him. He would watch the needle pierce his skin to find the vein while he chatted with the nurse and watched the dark blood fill all the test tubes she needed. He never showed any pain or fear during these procedures. The radiation was no different. Another adventure.

Dressed again in his own clothes, he looked none the

worse for the experience. The deterioration would start from the inside. Invisible.

The night the marrow came, I was not there. It was Dtaw's turn to be with Chan. Christmas. My mom had flown out from Maine and brought a small artificial tree and a pile of beautifully wrapped presents for Chan's spacious room. The transplant rooms were the nicest in the hospital. A picture window provided a view of an enclosed green space beyond which treetops stretched into the distance. When I looked out, I could never orient myself geographically. I never knew where we were. I sometimes wondered what was beyond the trees in the distance, but I gave up quickly. It didn't matter.

The nights I couldn't sleep from worry, from feeling Chan's feverish skin next to mine in the narrow bed with its hard chrome rails, I would lie down on the window seat, shutting my eyes against the blue-white monitor lights and red numbers always glowing beside him. I would sleep in small pieces between nurses coming in and out to check blood pressure and pulse through the night.

In the daytime, Chan loved to sit with me on the window seat and play with the collection of small stuffed animals he'd gathered, some provided by the hospital, some gifts from friends. Dividing them into two facing teams, he would line them up on the window seat. "Let's play war, Mama." I'd sit behind my team making funny voices for the different animals. My team was led by a bumbling general who yelled at his men to advance but always to their doom, as Chan's floppy ponies and eagles and puppies pounced on mine, gaining unequivocal victory every time as I howled in defeat. He never tired of that game.

Dtaw and I alternated nights with him. I was there with him in the daytime and every other night. I sat with him listening, holding, soothing, while he suffered the itching, nausea, and pain. But the night they put the new marrow in his blood, I wasn't there.

It arrived after midnight, flown in from far away. They had told us earlier that day it was on its way, so we had been anticipating its arrival like that of a faraway friend. Dtaw took pictures, catching Chan's smile bright, everlasting. He poses beside the small IV bag of liquid, a bulging bag of gold, like honey, that the nurse holds in her hands. The marrow will enter the blue-capped side of the double-headed line that snakes into Chan's heart. His smile shines, knowing, having been told, that this is what will save his life.

WISHES

I HURRIED DOWN THE NARROW STAIRWAY of our two-bedroom apartment, flip phone pressed to my ear as I listened to the message from the Make-A-Wish volunteer. He had called so many times asking to meet that his voice had taken on an apologetic tone. I had ignored all his messages.

I was rushing to get Cody and Tahn packed into our minivan. Visiting hours would start shortly, and I hated to have Chan miss a minute with his brothers. Splitting up at the end of the day, alternating one parent at home, one at the hospital, was near the top of our list of what we didn't like about living with leukemia.

"I was just calling again to see if we could find a time to come over to talk to you and your husband about Chan's Make-A-Wish." He pronounced *Chan* like everyone who didn't know him did, with a long *a* sound instead of short, rhyming it with *man* instead of *John*. I listened almost all the way to the end of the message before closing the phone. With all I had to worry about, helping Chan recover from the recent transplant and trying to keep Cody, now seven, and Tahn, two, fed and happy, sitting down with a stranger to talk about something that didn't have a direct impact on Chan's survival was low on my priority list.

"Come on, guys, let's go!" I called out to my boys, trying to sound cheerful and patient. Cody was already zipping his little brother into the lime-green padded coat I had gotten in one of the bags of hand-me-downs our friends brought when we first arrived. Tahn was trying to wriggle away, but Cody, after only a few months as the oldest brother in a family whose predictable routines had been interrupted by serious illness, had learned fast how to bring things in his world under control. He spoke firmly to Tahn as he pushed the red mittens over Tahn's little fingers and marched him out to the minivan without any assistance from me. I was busy gathering up the daily doses of steamed broccoli and fresh vegetable juice to bring to Chan.

A few weeks later, after seven months of treatments and the bone marrow transplant, Chan was discharged from the hospital. The nurse showed me how to use the pill organizer that held the thirty-six pills he had to swallow each day. We found a daily routine that incorporated flushing his line, taking a walk, going to the playground, eating broccoli and whatever other foods Dtaw had, in his research, found to be antioxidants. We learned how to protect the hole in his chest with a large plastic sticker made especially for covering wounds for bathing, so we could give him quiet baths, careful, always careful to keep the bacteria-laden water from dripping close to any wrinkle in the sticker. When I found a free moment in the midst of all this, I returned the Make-A-Wish phone call and agreed to a time when the volunteer could come over.

* * *

We sat by the big window with its view of the twin apartment building across the wide lawn. Tahn wiggled on my lap, his bare bottom warm on my belly. Only recently weaned, he still took every opportunity to maintain skin-to-skin contact, and today this meant shoving his little feet up under my shirt and vigorously massaging my chest with his heels. I held his hands as he lay back against my thighs. His playfulness exhausted me. I felt my lower lip crack and bleed again as I smiled at the pleasure he took in his own mischief. I was so tired and distracted during those months of Chan's treatment, so intent on taking care of him, that there was no time for me to remember to drink water. I grabbed a tissue to soak up the blood.

The volunteer looked away and watched the boys playing in the area between us. The living room was only a small space by the front door with love seat and soft chair between the window and the kitchen. It was also our playroom. Cody and Chan, dressed as Ninja warriors, fought with plastic swords between us. His head still shiny and bald, swathed in black polyester scarves revealing only his eyes, Chan jumped and parried with his big brother as if he'd never been sick. Finally, I pulled him over to sit next to me to answer the volunteer's questions.

"Mom, can you untie me? I'm sweaty." Chan turned his back to me and I gently loosened and released the knots at the nape of his neck.

With Chan standing still, the volunteer saw his opportunity and asked, "What would be the one thing you'd want more than anything right now? If you could have one wish, what would it be?"

"A horse. A black scallion."

"Okay." The volunteer made a note on the legal pad he held on his lap.

"And if you couldn't have that, what would you want?"

"My cousin Jew to come."

The volunteer paused before asking again, "Okay, what else?"

"An Xbox."

I was disappointed. Since we'd made the Make-A-Wish appointment, I'd been priming Chan. I knew it wasn't right, but I couldn't stop myself. I would casually mention ideas that appealed to me and my fantasies of escape. "Honey, what about a snowboarding vacation in Utah? Doesn't that sound like fun?" When I got no enthusiasm for that, I tried others. "Don't you want to go to Hawaii? You could surf." After the last time he shook his head and replied with finality, "A black scallion," I gave up trying.

The volunteer returned to our living room three weeks after his first visit with the verdict on Chan's wishes. "We can't get you a horse. We would have to find a place for it outside of Seattle, and with the costs and complications involved in stabling it and getting you to and from the place with your suppressed immune system, it's just not practical long-term."

Chan listened without visible concern and immediately responded, "What about Jew?"

The volunteer shifted in his seat and looked down at his legal pad before responding: "Well, international visas are not something we get involved with. So we won't be able to do that either."

Chan waited, knowing he didn't need to remind the volunteer about his next wish.

"As far as the Xbox, your parents have forbidden that." (Okay, so I didn't give up all my rigid beliefs about wholesome parenting.) "But we were able to compromise on a plan. We are getting you a laptop you can use for non-violent games and later for your education."

Chan looked at me. I shrugged. I wanted to say, *See, I told you you should have gone for the snowboarding vacation.* He wasn't surprised he didn't get the Xbox. He knew his father and me well enough to know we would never let him have a large chunk of polar-bear killing plastic dedicated to games that required neither large motor movement nor human interaction.

"Thanks," he told the volunteer, and went upstairs to play Legos with Cody.

The laptop arrived in the mail a week later. A flat black computer that, at the time, seemed state-of-the-art. It weighed close to ten pounds.

Dtaw and I kept it on the desk in our bedroom. The Make-A-Wish people had installed video games they thought we'd approve of. We did. The one we all loved involved virtually riding a BMX dirt bike over desert scenes. We would intentionally fly off cliffs and over huge jumps. The air time was exciting, and when you crashed, you never died. You could just keep playing.

~~~

NEWS

~~~

WHEN THE NURSE FROM THE HOSPITAL CALLED, nine months after we'd come to Seattle for treatment, I wasn't expecting any remarkable news. Chan had been doing well. He was getting stronger every day; he roughhoused with his brothers and ran in the grass outside the apartment like a normal healthy boy. I was having conversations with the social worker about his eventual return to school.

"The routine aspirate showed blasts in the peripheral blood," the nurse's voice at the other end came, quiet but resigned.

"What are blasts?"

"Immature cells." She sounded grim. I didn't understand why. Then she said something about the elephant in the room.

"What elephant?"

"The cancer is back. The transplant failed." Her voice indicated she was trying to soften the blow of delivering this news, but I could hear her own sense of failure.

"Oh." I felt my heart sink as I lowered myself onto the chair behind my knees.

"Chan is in relapse."

I was unable to register this as fact until the next day when we met with Chan's transplant doctor. Dtaw and I sat in a dim conference room across the table from the doctors, social worker, and a few other members of Chan's medical team. I felt sorry for the oncologist. He was so young to be facing such a hard situation, telling parents that their child was incurable. When the meeting began, he turned to us and, in a controlled voice and with face drawn in regret, explained the situation. He made it clear: Chan would not live. The hospital would continue to support him with morphine and transfusions as long as he needed them. Any alternatives would only prolong his pain and suffering.

The doctor outlined the options, never quite meeting our gaze. Or maybe mine wasn't meeting his. "In these situations, the cancer is never successfully eradicated. You could choose to have Chan undergo another transplant, but most likely that will only extend and intensify his suffering."

He went on to illustrate his point by telling us the details of a patient who lived for months longer in the hospital but with terrible, painful complications from the treatment. The doctor was so against further treatment that we agreed to let the disease follow its natural course, our only prospect being palliative care. I asked the doctor to define what this meant.

"When Chan's suffering becomes unbearable, we will introduce morphine and increase the doses until death takes away his pain."

I asked him how much longer Chan had to live.

"We don't like to try to predict that. It varies from patient to patient."

"Well, are we talking years or months?" I pressed.

He hesitated before replying, "He might have as much as two months."

I don't clearly recall my emotional state after this meeting. I don't think I had one. I was simply numb. I do remember being accepting and obedient. "Chan will die," I tried to tell Dtaw when we got home. I knew he would not accept the doctor's prediction, so I spoke in my most please-be-reasonable-and-well-behaved voice.

But Dtaw is usually neither of those things. He insisted that we neither obey nor believe the doctors, but that we pack up our family and fly straight back to Thailand to fight for Chan's life as hard as we possibly could where he knew of people who would believe in Chan's ability to heal himself.

At first I thought this was unreasonable and unrealistic. I thought we needed to accept Chan's fate, be rational, calm, dignified adults. But over the course of that night, as I listened to Dtaw's conviction that Chan deserved our support in fighting for his life, that there were people in Thailand who could help, something old and seemingly intractable inside me began to shift. I began the slow turning toward hope that required a kind of strength I had never felt wakening before.

We left Seattle with our doctors' blessings.

PART 4

BACK TO BANGKOK

CODY SCANNED THE BAGGAGE CLAIM AREA while I stood dazed from heat and twenty hours trapped in flight with three busy boys and a sleeping husband. "Over there, Mama. Number three." At eight years old and after nine months of living with his brother's illness, Cody had become the family expert at logistics. Seeing his father and me too absorbed in caring for Chan to be able to think clearly about getting from point A to B, Cody was taking up the slack. Serious-and-efficient had settled onto his little-boy self like a second skin. Now, nearly midnight after a long journey and a whirlwind week of packing and saying goodbye to his Seattle world, he heaved his small body back in counterbalance to the weight of a sluggish metal cart from the line between the baggage carousels and, pushing into it, led the way. The two of us maneuvered the eight enormous duffle bags and four carry-ons onto three carts. Dtaw's back was bad, so Cody and I always did the heavy lifting. But Dtaw could push a cart. Chan and Tahn sat perched atop one of the piles of luggage, and the customs man waved us through.

Hours later, drunk with jet lag, we were still awake at three a.m., sitting around Dtaw's sister Jum's kitchen table eating leftover noodles and slapping at hungry mosquitoes. Sticky and tired, it was hard to feel we'd made the right choice coming to such a hot, dirty city.

When it was finally dawn, we bathed in the cold water from the cistern, the children laughing and splashing with Jew as they always did. Mei Ya hurried us along so that we could get to the temple to see about getting Chan's cure underway first thing. All nine of us crowded into Jum's small sedan, and headed into Bangkok rush hour, traveling to the temple where the monk most influential in matters of health presided.

Chan had always loved temple visits. When he was a baby, and we rode our bicycles through the countryside, we often stopped at a temple to rest. The white thick-walled structures offered cool air inside and deep shade outside. Red-tiled rooftops swept toward the heavens, apexes tipped with long golden serpent heads that drew our eyes and thoughts upward. The grounds were always swept clean by the monks to ensure that they did not crush the life out of any bug too small to see as they walked. And flowers and trees rose succulent and abundant from the dry earth, offering serenity and color.

On those visits, before exploring the gardens, we first entered the main hall where we paid homage to the Buddha's teachings and the monks who lived there. All of us on our knees, Cody and Jew even as toddlers knowing well what to do, we faced first the large golden statue of the Buddha that was the focal point of every temple, touching our foreheads and palms to the floor three times before doing the same as we turned to bow to whatever monk happened to be there. Then we would fall into quiet talk with the most senior monk present.

On the way to the Bangkok temple that morning, we stopped at the market to buy stews, meats, and sweets to offer the monks. When we arrived and the monks had seated themselves cross-legged on the raised platform at the front of the room, Chan placed the food into the begging bowls lined up before the men, old and young, dressed in dark yellow robes. As we moved down the line on our knees, the monks reached out and touched Chan's head, smiling encouragement for our sick little boy.

The monks began chanting, and when it came to the time in the ceremony to bless the water each supplicant had brought, Dtaw helped Chan hold Mei Ya's special brass pitcher as they poured it into the matching cup. Then everyone went outside to pour the holy water on the roots of the Bodhi Tree, the tree of enlightenment and symbol of the Lord Buddha. It was under this tree in Bodh Gaya, India, that the Buddha, after years of practice and seeking, is said to have achieved enlightenment. The monks believed that the huge tree at the temple was started from a cutting brought from the Buddha's tree.

As Chan poured holy water over the tree's huge tangle of roots, each of us reached out and touched him, as is the custom, gently placing fingertips and palms on his skin, sharing the giving and receiving of blessing that the ceremony signified. Chan smiled, happy to be at the temple, at home, with the family he'd missed.

A few weeks later, Chan was hospitalized when graft-versus-host disease (GVHD) set in. As we'd decreased his immunosuppressant medication and his original mar-

row began to fight against the donor marrow as a foreign invader, the condition of GVHD arose. This was a
good thing because if the donor marrow won the battle,
eradicating the cancer-producing marrow, the transplant
would be a success. The problem was that GVHD could
be not only extremely debilitating and painful, but also, if
left to rage for too long, fatal. The doctor said we would
be playing "cat and mouse" with the disease until he felt
it was too dangerous for Chan, and then he would administer steroids to halt the progression of the fight inside
Chan's body.

Our hospital room faced east. I should say Chan's.
He reminded me that it was his room, his bed, when I
wouldn't let him do what he wanted, usually watch TV.
*I should let a dying boy watch cartoons that make him
laugh*, I thought. I did some of the time, but too much of it
seemed only to make him feel worse. I supposed coming
back into the pain in his body after the escape into the
world of television was overwhelming.

Chan had been in the hospital for two weeks. Because
Thailand has universal health care for its uninsured cit-
izens, medical bills were not something we had to worry
about. Public hospitals were almost free, and even luxu-
rious private hospitals were a fraction of the cost of US
hospitals. Now Chan, thinner than ever before from the
havoc that GVHD was wreaking in his gut, lay on his bed
in one of Bangkok's best private hospitals, groaning, "*Kow
neeyow*" (sticky rice), his favorite food. He hadn't eaten
since he'd been checked in.

Outside the setting sun sent its last brightness across
the skyscrapers, lighting up the glass sides against the dark

gray backdrop of early night sky beyond. Close enough for me to see figures moving behind each window as electric lights switched on against the night. On balconies, laundry racks shifted left or right as people pulled in shirts and underwear, stiff and warm, at the end of another hot, sunny day. I could not see well into the golden rooms, but I could make out furniture and lamps and kitchen counters and people with their own lives and pain and love. So many cells in the immense tall honeycombs. So much for one flimsy structure of cement and steel to contain.

But the city night's soft air warmed my bare arms. From our seventh-floor balcony, where I stood whenever I could escape Chan's bedside, I surveyed the by-now-familiar nighttime scenes below. A building, half-constructed, supported dozens of workers, like ants busy on a dry mound. In the daytime they were invisible behind the green plastic mesh that shaded them, but at night the glow of a long white fluorescent bulb set the stage for a man working on the bones of the structure behind the green scrim. Below, dwarfed by the first levels of the high-rise, another man bathed behind his once-white cement house, now gray from the exhaust that spewed from cars and trucks all day. In the cool of the darkness, he poured bowls of water over his nearly naked body to wash away the grime of a day's labor in the smog-shrouded city. Nearby, a television screen flashed incessantly at another man repairing the blue ceramic tiles of his roof. To the right at the construction site, a huge funnel-shaped vat for cement slid on an invisible wire from ten stories up to the street below. The workers' spotlight threw a finely detailed shadow of the man's figure across the mesh.

As the sky darkened, the man on the roof disappeared

down a ladder, his TV and tools gathered by the gutter. The construction worker, bareheaded and wearing flip-flops, picked up the glowing rod of light and carried it, cord trailing, to another room beyond my sight. If I could go there, I could find him by its glow, I thought. Through a window frame a hundred feet down and opposite the hospital, the silver ring of a cooking spoon circled in a black wok.

Back in our room Chan lay on his side, the curve of his hipbone sticking out above the rest of his body. The caricature of a skeleton we saw every day on *Scooby-Doo* or *Popeye* was taking over the shape of his once-perfect little-boy body. This was one of the hardest parts for me, this thinness.

Three weeks after waiting out the disease, when the doctor witnessed the pain that tore through Chan's gut, he decided that the battle inside his body had to be put to an end. He administered the steroids. The healthy donor marrow had been defeated. Chan's own marrow, producing cells that were multiplying and could gather to kill him, had won.

However much I begged and pushed and cajoled, Chan would not come out to the balcony to feel the air and see the world. He preferred to hide in the bed he'd occupied for weeks, with the sound and sight of Daffy Duck beaming down from the TV mounted on the ceiling. I asked him one more time to come out and see the view and was refused again. I sighed and gave up. I left him alone and slipped back outside to warmth and darkening sky. Some tiny clouds floated by, ghostly white, undersides lit up by city lights, and I was surprised to see a sprinkling of stars above.

LEAVING BANGKOK

OUR HOUSE STOOD QUIET, with only the rumble of faraway trucks and airplanes and the whispering of a string of paper Ninja Turtles fluttering at the window. Chan was finally sleeping and Tahn too. I thought of how the night before Chan had had enough pain in his ankle from the infection that if we'd been in the hospital, they would have convinced me that he needed a big IV push of morphine. Then he'd be on a continuous drip by now, sleepy, muddled, and unable to do the work of getting well or at least of fighting his way to feeling better. I didn't think morphine let your body heal in the best way possible.

The week before, when I'd told the doctor over the phone that Chan's eyelid was red and puffy, he had said, "Hmm, sounds like the leukemia has infiltrated the eyelid." The next day it was fine. Would it have infiltrated and then left? It seemed like whatever symptom I told the doctors about, they interpreted as another section of the downward slide, with no hope of reversal. But Chan was walking on his own after the infection in his foot that had him hospitalized and near death for a week. He'd told me that morning he'd tried running. "I looked like a dog with a broken leg," he reported. Dtaw told me he had soaked it with ginger compresses in the night. The doctor thought the infection and pain and misery were irreversible. Yet Chan was better. He had been so thin, but I could see more meat on his bones and an insatiable appetite. I had to work so damn hard to keep believing in life, in the ability of the body to heal itself rather than falling so easily prey to the hopeless discouraged attitude of the doctors.

"We're not going to cure him. Just give him more morphine. Don't increase his misery with unnecessary treatment." This was what the doctor told me when I kept insisting he call in a specialist about the pain in Chan's foot, the fever, and the swelling. The doctor had seen too many parents keep their dying children alive through painful complications of leukemia, and he didn't want us to do the same to Chan. We had a different outlook.

I tried to find other doctors who would see things our way. "Oh, he's post-transplant relapse?" they asked. "Why are you bothering to treat? This is simply another sign of his demise." They all had the same hopeless attitude. There was no room for the idea that Chan might surprise us all and heal. I couldn't stand to meet with one more doctor who looked at me as if I were crazy, asking for their help, when clearly my child was terminal. Nothing they could do.

We still wanted to fight, so after six months of working to get Chan well in Bangkok and too many hospital visits for transfusions and treatment of infection, we decided it was time to go. The doctors didn't want us to leave Bangkok. The allopathic doctor was sure Chan's blood cells would fail in a matter of days. "Why don't you just go for a week-end to the countryside to visit his relatives, say goodbye. Then come back here for platelets and red blood cells."

The nutritionist frowned and shook his head. "Why? We can continue the megadoses of vitamins here. Stay six more months to build his strength, and then go."

But we were determined to take Chan where we thought he would be happier. He spoke every day of living on the mountain with horses Dtaw would bring from Laos. He wanted to see Mei Tong and live in our cabin so high up that eagles flew below us across the valley. We were all tired of Bangkok with the smog and traffic and too many doctor's appointments and hopeless faces.

And the doctors didn't have anything to offer besides transfusions and morphine. We didn't think Chan was ready for all that yet. We had faith his body could fight. The blood counts the doctors relied on for information didn't seem to tell us much. Up and down the numbers went each week, so that the predictions I had believed so many times (*the blasts are down—he's getting well; the blasts are up—he's dying*) had become pointless.

We decided to go where Chan wanted to be, where we hoped that clean air, pure water, and proximity to the healing energy of nature might bring back what man-made toxins and pollutants and radiation had damaged, perhaps beyond repair. We left Bangkok to return to the home on the river where he'd been born, to gather up our things, to find the horses, and to prepare for the move to the mountains.

Chan was delighted to leave Bangkok. That morning, so early it was still dark, he eagerly got up to get dressed. It was the first day in three weeks of extreme pain in his foot that he was able to run around and play with his brothers. While Dtaw and Cam and I put the final boxes into the waiting truck, Chan and Cody and Tahn laughed loudly as they marched up and down the stairs chanting at the top of their lungs, "You can't *be* hard core unless you *live* hard core!"

~~~

GATHERED

~~~

T HE COOL MIST ROLLED DOWN THE LANE from the river in the early-morning dark as if to welcome us home. We pulled up in front of our house after the all-night journey from Bangkok. With the help of the neighbors, we unloaded the eight-wheeled truck that had followed us with our belongings. Bicycles, furniture, clothes, Champion juicer ordered from America, extra-virgin olive oil purchased from the only health food store in Bangkok—all were carried into the house amid laughter and talk about where we'd been and what we'd missed. No one looked at us with pity or worry. Our friends knew how to stay focused on the present without visible concern for the future or acknowledgment of the problem. Even when Chan was not within earshot, Dtaw's friends would not bring up his illness until Dtaw did. It was not avoidance. It was generosity. It was tenderness, a willingness to wait, to leave curiosity unfed. It was also a way to be fully in the present without filling it with fears about the future. This skill was one cultivated over a lifetime of small-town life, I imagined. Giving those one lived with space to have their lives, their problems, without being pressed for action or explanation. Dtaw's friends were experts at this.

With the women, and especially with his mother, it was different. She was always worrying, asking, insisting on a response. And the less he gave her, the more she probed.

Dtaw called his oldest friends to meet him at the house that afternoon. One by one, they showed up after lunch until four of them were gathered listening, waiting to hear what he wanted.

"You need to go find a horse for Chan. A black stallion."

His friends waited for more. They did not exchange questioning looks. They did not speak. Their respect for Dtaw ran deep. He had led their gang of friends, more like brothers, since they were children. They would do anything he asked. He went on to explain that Chan wanted a horse—not just any horse, but a black stallion. They knew there were none to be found in this part of the country, so they continued to listen through the frequent long pauses in his speech they knew well from a lifelong friendship.

"You will need to go to the other side of the river and head north. Searching close to the border of China, you will find horses. They use them instead of buffalo for plowing and pulling carts in some villages there." There were few roads in Laos, a country of deep jungle and high mountains. Travel and trade was done mostly by boat along the Mekong. But there were some rough dirt roads trucks could rumble slowly over, in and out of deep gullies of mud and dust. The quest would involve patience and endurance.

After the instructions had been given, the men nodded, knowing that they would not come home until they had found what Chan wanted. Dtaw went back to the kitchen and came out with bottles of beer, an ice bucket, and glasses. Cody and Jew ran to help, Jew lifting the ice cubes, edges smoothed by the heat, with thin aluminum tongs to drop them into the glasses before Cody carefully poured the amber liquid almost to the brim for these men he called *Paw*, his other daddies. Their talk softened into laughter as they asked Tahn and Cody about life in America. Paw Tum held Chan in his lap, arms wrapped tight around his thin body. "This one I missed the most," he exclaimed, teasing Tahn and Cody that he didn't miss them as much. They were too big and tough now to love, he laughed. They laughed too.

Later in the afternoon, when the men had left and the house had quieted down enough for Chan and me to rest together on the cool cement floor, he turned to me and said, "I feel my power all the time. I feel like a tiger or something."

"I'm so glad, honey. That's so important. You need your power."

That evening, while Cody and Jew and Dtaw went to the schoolyard to play soccer in the cooling of the day, Chan and I took a walk by the river we had missed so much. As we stood gazing out at the red and orange clouds beneath the violet gray sky of sunset, he looked up at me and said in a quite matter-of-fact way, "I hope I don't die when I'm a kid."

"Why not?" I asked, only to keep him talking.

"Because I don't want to die yet."

I smiled on the outside.

The next morning, our first back at home, I awoke before the other four, cuddled on the pallet we all slept on. Packed hard with the downy fluff of kapok pods that hung at the tops of tall trees beside the house, it made a good bed for all of us. Carefully disentangling myself from the sweet softness of my three boys' skinny thighs and warm breath, I pulled the blanket back over them before climbing out from under the mosquito net and standing up to absorb a moment of solitude before my day began. The mist that settled shortly after midnight blurred the light of the waning moon. The crickets' chirping and roosters' calls would have made it hard to sleep had I not been used to them. Downstairs the glow from the streetlight shone in slender straight lines through the gaps in the planks of the walls. The bathroom floor tiles were cold but dry under my bare feet.

Back upstairs I tried to go back to sleep. It felt too early to be up, only a little after four, although all our neighbors had been up for hours readying the goods they made and sold each day in the market. Their preparations began early every afternoon. Whenever I looked out my window into the neighbors' yard after lunch, I saw the grandfather roasting a pig's snout, its skin blistering white and black, as the old man sat smoking a fat cigar of rolled-up leaves beside the fire. The snout would become part of the sausages, stuffed and hung, festooning their outdoor kitchen, until taken to sell at the morning market.

The market was the town's social center. There every day under the glow of bare lightbulbs strung over outdoor stalls in the morning dark, neighbors met and chatted. Doughnuts floated in vast woks of bubbling oil while buyers waited for them to be scooped out, drained, and rhythmically snatched with long chopsticks and put into plastic bags lined with squares of paper, children's cut-up worksheets from school. Sausages lay pink and plump coiled on aluminum trays before the fat gregarious women who sold them beside boiling pots of fresh soy milk flavored with *bai toey*, pandanus leaves, fragrant green blades of what looked to me like dune grass stems. Every morning we walked through, carrying our baskets, laughing and chatting with the many neighbors and cousins we saw, carefully selecting the best vegetables and cuts of meat to cook for our family.

At this early hour, the monks at the temples had been long awake, chanting together in the dark, then sweeping their long twig-bundle brooms in graceful arcs across the hard-packed dirt of the temple grounds just as the sun began to rise. Before it got above the horizon, they picked up their begging bowls, twisted the free end of their robes into a rope to tug over their shoulders, and set off barefoot to collect their morning meal.

Whenever we woke early enough, Chan was eager to go to the end of our little lane to be with his grandmother as she put fistfuls of sticky rice into the monks' bowls as she had done every morning for most of her life. Even his great-grandmother, at ninety-nine years old, still got up before the sun every morning to light her cooking fire and steam rice and packets of meat and vegetables she wrapped in shiny green leaves to offer to the monks. Squatting in front of her house, wrinkled, stick-like legs doubled up under her, she waited. Swathed in white cotton sarong, layered shirts, and bundled in scarves and a yellow knit cap, she watched for the lines of monks to come down the lane, one group from each of the seven temples in the town, and some from outside of the town too, their bare feet silent on the road as they approached. When Dtaw's grandfather died more than ten years earlier, his wife had shaved her hair close to her head and vowed to wear only white to show that, as a widow, she would faithfully follow the eight precepts taught by the Lord Buddha.

At home my family slept. Soon I knew I would hear the anguished cries of "Mama!" as if they could not bear to be in bed without me. Usually it was Chan who called out first. No wonder of course; we had been so terrified for him for the past fourteen months. But back in our home after those long months away, close to a year, I was beginning to relax and think he might be getting well. He was happy to be home, laughing and playing and trying to run, bugging his dad every day to buy him a bike. He refused to ride the one he had because he said it wasn't big enough. His ankle was still swollen from the infection he had in Bangkok, but without much pain, he said.

When Chan woke up, he hurried me downstairs to sit with him while he built the fire in the coal-bucket stove in the yard. Using a sharp machete to split kindling into tiny sticks, he laid one atop the other, crisscrossing them, log-cabin style, before starting the blaze. There was a chill in the air, not too cold, but in our house mornings meant standing naked in the bathroom first thing and pouring bowls of cold water from the hip-high jar over our bodies. I was happy to have such a skinny boy warm up in front of a fire. Often Mei Ya stepped through the gate as we sat, bringing a fish to roast or a stew to cook slowly over the coals.

In the garden around us, edible vines twisted around

trunks of towering papaya trees that Dtaw, Chan, and Cody had planted when Tahn was born. Waking up to the thump of passion fruit on the clean-swept dirt meant that we could walk outside to pick up the shiny yellow-green balls for our breakfast. If we wanted to gather bounty from above rather than below, we could poke with a long bamboo stick at the papayas and star fruit hanging high.

That morning, when Mei Ya came to bring some chicken soup for breakfast, Chan told her he'd been wanting one of her special treats, banana and coconut milk sticky rice steamed in banana leaves. My mother-in-law, habitually cheerful, stout, and strong from raising six children and feeding her large extended family for most of her life, went into the lane and called over one of the neighborhood boys from where he sat with his friends. Pressing a silver coin into his hand, she told him to run to the market to buy some coconut. "Hurry, before Little Sister Nong rests from her morning work," she urged him. It was nearing seven a.m. and the market would soon be closing. The coconut seller, like many of her comrades, often stayed by her stall, stretched out on an empty table for a morning nap in case a late riser came to shop. But waking them up never felt right.

The neighbor was back in less than ten minutes. He stepped through the gate and handed over the plastic bag bulging with its treasure of bright white coconut flesh, oily, freshly scraped from its rough brown shell. Mei Ya took it from him without a word, and dumped all of it onto the wide enamel tray she had waiting. Then from the fire, she lifted the huge aluminum tea kettle and poured some of the boiling water over the coconut. With the ends of her fingers, she blended the water and flakes together until the mixture was cool enough to begin squeezing over a sieve, a tin bowl with holes nailed through the bottom. Jew and Cody came running to help. They dutifully washed their hands as they were told, knowing the coconut cream would not keep if contaminated with too much bacteria. They leaned over the tray beside their grandmother, five hands lifting, squeezing, as Mei Ya held the sieve under the rain of milk, *hua grati,* literally head of the coconut milk or coconut cream. A second round of squeezing and straining would produce a less rich liquid to be used in cooking, but it was the cream that she would use for Chan's treat.

Mei Ya went into the shed and returned lugging one of the family's larger woks, four feet in diameter. She settled it, heavy and solid, over the dancing fire and poured the cream in, stirring without ceasing as it heated. Cody wanted to remember how to make this next time, so he recited the recipe as he watched, narrating her movements of pouring the stream of white sugar into the swirling milk, then spooning the wet sticky rice into the liquid. After the rice had absorbed the sweet cream and been left to cool, Chan, Cody, and I, under Mei Ya's critical eye, spooned the rice into the centers of cut-up banana leaves. We then laid a quarter of a miniature banana on each little heap and folded the packet as instructed, skewering it tight together with toothpicks Mei Ya had split from a section of a hollow, jointed stem of bamboo. Finally, we placed the green pyramids carefully into the bamboo basket for steaming.

One bunch of bananas was the right amount for the rice and leaves she had prepared. A half hour later she took the lid off the basket and lifted the shiny dark treasures, covered in a sweat of condensed steam, out onto a plate. After they cooled enough to handle, we hurried to unwrap the packets and pop the warm treats into our mouths. Chan must have eaten ten packets over that day and the next morning. Nothing could have pleased me more.

In the coming days, I was busy as I had always been in our home, cooking, feeding, doling out vitamins and hugs, and being the referee when the boys fought. For the most part, they played well together with room to run around and neighbors to play games with in the lane. Dtaw kept the household running. In charge of the garden and trips to the market each day, he was always coming and going on the motorbike, bringing snacks of fresh-shaved coconut, pumpkin fudge, or toasted sticky rice. When he went on his errands, he called to Cody and Tahn to hop on the seat behind him, giving me short breaks from their needs. All of our energy and attention went into working to get Chan well. When we returned to Thailand, Dtaw had sold a piece of his family's land. This provided money to cover our modest expenses of food and gas. The rice hut at the farm was full of the year's harvest, the vines that twisted around the fence were abundant with leafy greens, and the trees were loaded with papayas and mangoes and passion fruit. We had enough.

We'd only been back a few days before I noticed that eight-year-old Cody was already a leader in the games of tag and dodgeball and soccer among the boys and girls on the street. Tahn played with them too, barefoot, as I could not get him to keep his shoes on in the dusty road despite the sticky black chicken droppings and flattened luckless lizards and large bugs. Even at two, he pointed out that all the big kids took their shoes off when they played. It was true. And flip-flops are not as good as bare feet for running. I didn't worry about him, though. There were enough older children and grown-ups out that I could concentrate on cooking or unpacking or tending to Chan.

It pained me that Chan could not join in the children's games because I had let the infection in his foot get out of control. If only I had gotten him the antibiotics sooner, he could have been running and playing too. So many decisions, so many points along this road where I took the wrong turn as his illness gained the advantage. It was natural for me to torture myself with regret, so I had to actively work not to dwell there. By then I had made it a habit to remind myself that the damage, whether from lingering infection or growing leukemia, would not be permanent. Nothing in the body is permanent. There is no inevitable downward slide as the doctors were so fond of believing. Every moment the body recreates itself. Cells are dying and renewing themselves all the time. The opportunity for health is unlimited, I kept telling myself.

So, not too long after we'd arrived, I gave in to Chan's repeated requests that he accompany his brothers and friends to the river to play in the cool mud. Since his treatment had begun, he had been mostly in hospital rooms or at home, isolated from anyone outside the family. Now that the medical world had given up hope for his recovery, we were making our own decisions about his care. So at last, I let him play with friends despite the risk of infection.

As he dug in the sticky mud for the first time, I dutifully reminded him about the danger of bacteria. I didn't have the heart to stand my ground when he argued that he was being careful.

Chan loved to go riding over the dirt roads in the 1966 Land Rover Dtaw had bought when Cody was a baby. One evening, Dtaw took the boys and they drove to a beautiful bend in the river where mountains rise up above the rapids that swirl around the rock formations disturbing the usually quiet surface of the water. When they came home, Chan ran to me and reported, wide-eyed and breathless, "Mama, we saw bats and the place in the river where the giant sleeps!"

As he spoke, I watched his pale lips, comparing his cousins' cherry-red to his own sometimes gray mouth. Other times his mouth looked almost pink. He seemed to have plenty of energy. Energy level is the real indicator of red blood cell deficiency, not coloring, I told myself. He was hungry. He cried and complained as any six-year-old would who'd been through what he had. I chose to be pleased with his health, for the time being.

He was adamant that we hurry up and get the horse he'd been asking for.

~~

BRUISE

~~

ONE MORNING ROUGHLY A WEEK AFTER our arrival back home, Dtaw asked, "Have you seen Chan's chest?"

"No, what?"

Chan stood before me, his knobby knees and ankles revealing the voracious wasting of the leukemia. He lifted his mesh soccer shirt. There, toward the center of his chest and above the scar from where the rubber line for the chemo had emerged above his heart, was a faint green bruise the size of a quarter, a perfect circle, like a stain from a drop of ink on white cloth. Stretching away from the spot were two blue spidery veins, like highways from a capital heading northeast and northwest in bumpy lines. I closed my eyes and leaned back against the porch railing in an effort not to faint from the wave of terror I felt breaking over me.

When I'd recently spoken to the doctor in Seattle on the phone, he told me petechiae, the tiny red freckles that indicate broken capillaries from platelet deficiency, do not need to be taken care of immediatcly. Spontaneous bruising does.

At my insistence, because I felt we needed to know what we were getting into by taking Chan into the mountains, far from medical care, the doctor had described in detail what death from low platelets would look like. Hemorrhaging in the brain would end Chan's life within a few minutes. A fatal nosebleed would go on for hours and be "uncomfortable" and "unpleasant" and "distressing" because of all the draining fluid. Bleeding in the bowels would be very painful.

I returned my attention to Chan. "Oh, it's nothing. He probably got bonked. Did you get bonked, honey?" I said, trying so hard to sound relaxed. I fought off the rising dizziness with huge breaths of air.

"Nope," he said, then noticed my breathing. "What's wrong, Mom?"

"Are you sure you didn't get hit yesterday? You've been running around a lot."

"No! I hate it when you do this, when you worry." His voice rose in agitation.

I held my head above the surface long enough to escape downstairs for a drink of water and a place to hide my worry from Chan. All our plans for a long life in the country with the horses he'd been dreaming of gave way to visions of hospital rooms, needles, blood tests.

Dtaw called down from upstairs to tell me that he was taking Tahn and Cody to the farm for the morning. This was so I could be left to concentrate on taking care of Chan. I opened the refrigerator and pulled out the pitcher of drinking water, poured a glass, and as I raised the cool liquid to my lips, I felt the relentless ghost of fear hovering at my side.

I saw my mind as a textbook example of Buddhist

theory. *Attachment is suffering.* When the child she loves is sick, the mother suffers from the pain of his pain and the fear that he will die. When he's well, she suffers from the fear that he will get sick and die. I lived always on the edge between desperate fear of his death on one side and joy and exultation at the thought of his getting well on the other. I could see the futility of always bouncing between these two points and always wondering if I'd be eternally happy or eternally brokenhearted. Of course, life never unfolds in such binary ways, good or bad, but I still couldn't stop myself from dwelling there on that brink, all sense of equanimity I thought I had succeeded in cultivating before Chan got sick, gone.

I tried to escape into dishes and laundry, but I could not get away from the fear. I moved about the house, trying to run from this feeling that everything was falling around me, that Chan would really get sick and die this time. I prepared a snack for him, going over in my mind the mental checklist: if this was his last week with us, were we doing what we should? He was back at home. He played with his friends all week. He was enjoying life. He was eating well. Were there any unresolved issues with members of his family I'd feel bad about if he died? No. His horse was on its way. I couldn't think of anything we should have been doing differently.

I was afraid the bruise meant that his platelets were so low that something was about to bleed uncontrollably. There was nowhere in Thailand to get platelets quickly. But more unsettling than the fear of imminent hemorrhage was the deeper fear that maybe we'd been completely wrong, that maybe the cancer really was growing wild, out of control. The ground I'd been standing on since our return home of, *Chan is doing so much better, Chan is stronger and happier every day, Chan is getting well,* dissolved under my feet.

Later, when Chan was asleep, I called my friend Maggie. She and I were part of a grassroots organization, a co-counseling community that encouraged connection and listening pairs in order to facilitate healing through emotional expression. In Seattle we met each week to share the struggles and joys of being mothers of young children. We had become efficient in talking to each other to get quickly to the meat of what was slowing us down, irritating us, making us feel stuck, as parents so often do. We split our time between being the listener and the speaker in a prescribed way that offered refreshing relief from the trials of mothering and engendered clearer thinking after our sessions.

"Maggie, this is just so damn hard. I'm so afraid he's dying. What do I do?" I asked, shaking and weeping while I talked, posing the unanswerable questions, naming the otherwise unspeakable fears there was no way to soothe. Maggie, patient and quiet, knew what I needed. She didn't answer my question. She listened without trying to fix. She let me release the thoughts I wasn't able to voice with anyone else. With her I could be hopeless and scared because I trusted her to stay hopeful for me. I allowed her to hold the armor of my courage for me while I cried, so that when I stepped back into being the brave mother, I could put it back on, refreshed from having rested from the weight of my role for a little while.

After talking with Maggie I realized that if Chan's death was imminent, he probably wouldn't have been so strong, hungry, and energetic. And if the bruise was something bad, we could at least wait and see if the next day it was bigger or smaller. If it got bigger, we'd take him to the doctor. If the bruise was from low platelets, and he did need a transfusion, then we'd get the blood product required. If it wasn't, we'd watch its progression, never analyzed or explained, another one of those things that his body did as it healed that we wouldn't understand because medical care at that point could not provide answers.

Either way, we had to plod along as we had been, keeping up the fight. That was the main thing: continuing to fight, no matter what the setbacks, just keep going and never give up. And fulfill Chan's biggest dream—to bring a horse to our home in the mountains and live there in our little cabin above the village.

Chan had fallen asleep on the wooden bridge under the thatch roof that rustled in the breezes between the sleeping and living buildings of our house on stilts. When he cried out in his sleep, I ran up to quiet him. I lay down next to him and he entwined his arms around me, pressing his face under my cheek, and locked me in with his thin leg thrown over my thigh. Soon he slept again. I resisted the urge to look at his chest. I had already examined Cody's for a control, checking for those visible blue veins, and I'd asked Dtaw to look at mine, but neither of ours was like Chan's. I told myself not to look again until the next day when he would undress for his shower.

Meanwhile, Dtaw had shared the news with me that not one, but *five* horses had made it to the village in Laos across the wide river. There they would rest a few days before swimming across to us. *How did one horse become five?* I asked myself. Dtaw figured Chan's brothers would need to ride too, so unbeknownkst to me, he had requested three. In the course of looking through the mountain villages where his friends had to beg the hill tribe people to part with one of the pack animals of their herd, they had found a black mare who had a six-month-old colt. Of course they couldn't resist her. And finally, after completing their mission of procuring three adult horses, but not of finding the object of their search, they came across a beautiful young stallion with a long bushy mane, all black.

My horse book said it is out of the question for beginners to own stallions. None of us knew the first thing about owning or training horses.

Even male colts are unmanageable and dangerous because of their hormones. All but the most experienced trainers own only mares and geldings, the book said. *And a beginner rider having a young horse to make friends with always ends in disaster.*

I asked Dtaw when he came home how many of the horses were males. All but one. Were any of them castrated? None.

BY THE RIVER

THE NEXT DAY CHAN WOKE PALE AND WAVERING. The bruise seemed to be fading. His leg hurt. He limped down the stairs and at breakfast said his knee was in pain as well, but it felt to him like toxins releasing. In the evening, Chan and Tahn and I walked down to the river to look at the green trees of Laos on the other side. We sat on the steps and wondered where the horses were and if Daddy and his friends would bring them down to the water for a drink. "Laos is so pretty," Chan said, "the trees and the mountains." Cody came and joined us. The boys picked up rocks to throw in the water or, in Tahn's case, at the cats by the water.

As we got up to leave the steps by the river and head back home, I noticed in the bright sunlight how very yellow Chan's skin was and how gray his lips were in comparison to his brothers. I felt another stab of panic looking at his pallor. I remembered the words of our neighbor as we passed her house on the way to the water: "Are you tired, Chan?" She used the Laotian word for fatigued, not sleepy, the word one would usually use with a child. I thought of how weak he had seemed recently. How he spent so much time lying down, how he napped of his own accord before noon, how weepy he was. And then the bruise, and I'd noticed a single red freckle on his jaw that morning, one of those tiny red spots the doctors called petechiae. He'd also started to complain of pain in his chin. The cough was hanging on, as was the cold. And now this yellowness.

That day it seemed so close at hand. That pallor, that weariness. *Maybe he is dying. Maybe the cancer is growing out of control.* These were the thoughts that plagued me all the next day when Dtaw was away. In the evening, I made Chan come stand out in the lane in front of the house where the children were playing some version of dodgeball. I wanted him to get up off the blanket on the floor where he had been resting all day. We stood in front of our gate, a safe distance from the children's game, while I fed Chan his favorite fruit, chunks of orange papaya.

"My legs are tired," he complained.

"I know. You seem tired today. I hope you don't need any more red blood cells," I mentioned in an offhand way.

He looked at me with familiar fear in his eyes. "You mean like by eating a lot of vegetables and drinking my juice, right?" His voice cracked as if he were holding back tears.

Oh, now what have I done? I've scared my child terribly.

"What do you mean, Mom?"

"No, I mean maybe you need a red blood cell transfusion to make you feel a little more energetic."

"I think I'm just tired because all I do is lie around all day. I don't play enough." His voice was still cracking with the strain of holding back his tears. "I just need to get a little more exercise. Then I won't be tired."

For the umpteenth time that day, I tried not to break down with the sorrow of seeing his worry. I hadn't realized the idea of going back to the cycle of doctors, hospitals, needles, and transfusions would be so upsetting. But of course it would. Why hadn't I thought before speaking?

When it was time to drink his juice and eat his vegetables, he faced the task with renewed commitment. How badly he wanted to stay away from the hospital, stay at home with his friends, and ride his horses in the country. Every day he kept drinking bitter juice and eating steamed dark green leaves and fighting for his right to live.

For me it was a fight too, a fight to keep up the struggle, no matter how scared and hopeless I got, to keep going. Because of the yellow, I was worried that his liver was overtaxed. I tried to remember the big picture, not get scared by the momentary frights. *So what if he's yellow? He was a bad color a year and a half ago, and he's been going strong since then. Some people just go through life looking sickly. He might grow up and still be yellow. That would be okay, as long as he grows up,* I told myself.

I was ashamed of how spiritually backward I seemed to be, so attached to one outcome. I thought I should have had more equanimity, ready to accept whatever happened. But the fact that I was naturally drawn to letting things go and not fight was exactly what kept me fighting. I knew that there was something wrong with the way I was pulled to give up and I realized that was not how humans were meant to act. And because it was my child, who I had to fight for, I had no choice but to do the right, the hard thing, which meant plugging along, day after day, trying to use my mind and heart to figure out what was best for him, whether or not to let him have soy milk that wasn't made of organic soy beans, whether to let him have dates when sugar was said to depress the immune system, vying with vitamin C for space in the cells. I had to not give up on figuring out how to get all his vitamins into him at the right time of day, how to make sure he got at least four glasses of freshly pressed, bitter juice a day, how to get the ginger and honey to him three times a day to fight the cough, to think about what else we could do to help him get over his cough, what else we could do to help him be healthy and live. It felt overwhelming so much of the time that I often did want to give up.

Cody asked me, whispering, that morning, "Can we eat doughnuts if we eat them at grandmother's house?"

I had to think. Chan might show up and want them and that wouldn't have been fair to him.

"I don't know the answer to that question!" I yelled, pent up frustration bursting out at my innocent eight-year-old. Then I sat down and calmed a bit. "No. The answer is no. If you want to eat junk food, you can't do it here. You'll have to go out."

BETTER

THE NEXT DAY WHEN DTAW DROVE OFF with Cody, Tahn, Cam, and Chan in the cab of the pickup truck, relief swept over me. Four whole hours to myself. No worries about getting Chan's juice, getting Chan's meds, making sure he had a nap, got enough to eat, got exercise and something to boost his spirits. Time just for me.

I was already pleased because Chan was looking so well. His face and lips were full. He was energetic and hadn't cried or complained or seemed listless all day. He'd eaten all the food we gave him with so little variation: steamed green leafy vegetables, steamed squash (like a miniature green pumpkin), steamed brown rice, grilled fish, fresh papaya, and four glasses of bitter vegetable and fruit juice. I was glad to be in a place where this (except for the juice) was regular fare that we could enjoy with Dtaw's mom and uncle, all eating together.

Chan was happy that morning because it was the day that he would finally go to the provincial capital, an hour drive away, to pick out a new bike. The one we'd bought six months before in Bangkok he still refused to ride because he said he'd outgrown it. Cody's old one, the next size up, he wouldn't ride because it didn't have gears. His favorite nurse in Seattle, a young Taiwanese-born American woman at Children's Hospital, gave him some red-envelope money for a going-away present, so he planned to use that for the new bike. He hadn't been able to go before because I wanted him to get over the cough and cold that had been bothering him.

He was also happy because the five horses his dad's friends had traveled to northern Laos to find for him had finally arrived at the village across the river. Tonight they would swim across the river to stay at Dtaw's uncle's farm before the journey to the mountains.

Dtaw had gone across the river to visit his friends and the horses after they returned from the north, and was pleased to discover the horses were gentle and well-trained (nobody had ridden them yet, but when Dtaw answered in the affirmative when I asked if he could walk up to them without them biting him, I was relieved). One man said that Mongolian horses were stronger than oxen or cows. He said during the war between the US and Vietnam, he had been a soldier for the Communist side. He had traveled through the high mountains in the roughest conditions with his small horse carrying loads of machine guns, ammunition, and supplies. A family who consented to sell one of their horses to our friends said it was used to pulling a cart carrying ten people over rough roads. And they all (except the colt, of course) had been used for plowing fields planted on steep hillsides.

So that chapter of our adventure would begin the next day. Chan was ecstatic, which delighted me.

The horses crossed the river, smuggled over by cousin

Gai's Laotian team and Dtaw's friends on the Thai side of the Mekong. Fearing police and border patrol on both sides, they managed to lead the five skittish creatures across the wide and deep expanse of dark cold water to the bank on the Thai shore, a few miles up from the village. Legs swept out from under them by the current, two of the horses' heads went under and a smuggler had to jump out of the slender, shallow-bottomed wooden boat and into the river. Pulling on the horses, dragging on the rope around their necks, they finally managed to get all five across.

The only female horse was pregnant and nursing a young foal. Easier to get across than the rest, they swam quickly and scrambled up the bank on the Thai side. The youngest stallion, Dtaw's friends told us later, blew like a drowning rhino, all the anxious way across, dogs barking, men sweating, outboard engine chugging. When he made it to shore, sides heaving, he rested there on the sandy bank before the men drove him up to the dark road.

The crossing took four hours and three trips back and forth across the wide river sweeping its dark path under the stars.

Creeping through town at two a.m., they worried that the neighing of the horses and barking of the village dogs would bring the police out of their roadside station, but they eventually made it to Gai's house where the horses were "stabled" in the backyard till morning. At two a.m., the smugglers came to our house to report on the operation, and Dtaw zoomed off on his scooter to a late-night restaurant to pick up hot takeout dishes. He hosted his friends with plenty of rice whiskey before they rested, napping on mats on the front porch in the hours before dawn. When they woke up a couple of hours later, shrugging off their sleepiness, they left to walk the horses the next two miles to the farm under cover of darkness.

I promised Chan that after breakfast we would go to the farm to see the horses. He was lying on the sheepskin, soaking in the morning sun, between Dtaw and me, while I massaged his back. I noticed the bruise was gone. He told me he'd just take a little snooze and I was to wake him when it was time to go. He fell asleep for at least an hour, uncharacteristic so soon after breakfast, and we tiptoed and whispered until he woke up. The sun became hot as it climbed in the sky, so I rigged up a shade by leaning a grass mat on its side against the cement pillar next to Chan. I fanned away the flies from his skin while I fretted over him.

Then I went to the kitchen to wash dishes at our outdoor sink.

Not much later I heard Chan's bare feet brush the smooth cement floor as he positioned himself to sit up. He immediately turned toward his dad. "I dreamed there was a huge mama horse and her baby and lots of elephants, one in back of the kitchen, some here, some in the garden."

"How big were the horses?" I called to him, hoping to squeeze as much joy out of a rare moment of enthusiasm as I could.

"Huge!" he shouted. "I couldn't even see their heads—they reached all the way to the sky! And the elephants were big too!"

Finally, a good dream.

MEETING THE HORSES

~~~

*T*HE FAMILY FARM LAY AT THE EDGE OF TOWN. A thirty-acre piece of land that, Dtaw often reminded me, was nothing compared to the vast tracts of lush riverside land his grandparents had once owned. Had his grandparents not given so much of it away to family and neighbors over the years, the land would have been worth millions of dollars now. His great-grandfather had been the village headman and Dtaw's grandmother told stories of being a very young girl and playing jacks, tossing and rolling the nuggets of gold the people of the neighboring towns brought to her father.

What was left to Dtaw and his cousins on his mother's side was this small piece by the road. We often escaped there for a quiet place to rest and pick mangoes or jackfruit or tamarinds. Farmers lived on the land to raise rice for his mother's household and their own.

The day we rode the motorcycle out to see the horses, the sun beat down hot, and the sharp dead ends of the grass poked our legs. Dtaw instructed me not to let the children come close to the scruffy little horses cropping the grass by the barbed-wire fence. He wanted to know better how tame they were before we ventured near. I kept the children close by me as we watched the horses from twenty yards away. The boys were disappointed that they didn't get to pet the horses right away.

"All we do is stand around and watch the grown-ups having fun," Cody assessed the situation with his usual realism. Chan gave into his misery over his dreamed-of black stallions turning out to be small, ragged-looking creatures that he couldn't even ride yet and began to cry.

At last I gathered my courage and picked him up to bring him close to the mare, giving her dangerous hind end a wide berth. We stepped forward and Chan stretched out his hand. She patiently endured his small fingers rubbing the short fur against the bone of her brow. He smiled.

We stayed long enough for each of the children to pet the mare and admire her colt, too skittish to let us touch him. When we got hungry, we laid a mat on the grass so we could slice and pound the green papaya Dtaw picked for us into a spicy sour salad to eat with the sticky rice we'd brought from home.

Later in the afternoon, back at the house, I was looking at the horse book Dtaw had brought home. Chan came to lie down next to me and decided it was time for a nap. I asked if he wouldn't rather go downstairs where we usually rested as it would be cooler.

"No, just here," he said, and was soon fast asleep. I watched the pulse in his neck as it seemed to beat wildly, and I thought about the risk of heart failure from low red blood cells because of the extra work required on the part of the heart to keep enough oxygen flowing throughout the body.

I went downstairs to find Cody's stop watch, and with some difficulty located a regular pulse in Chan's wrist. After I figured out that pressing the vein too hard against the bone caused a false rhythm, I was finally able to take a somewhat accurate reading: fifty-nine beats per thirty seconds. *That's okay*, I thought. But later I called the hospital about getting a blood draw and red blood cells. I talked to the pediatrician who had been the first to tell me about the possibility of leukemia. It had been only a year since we'd last spoken, but it felt like so much longer. So much had changed.

I went back upstairs to lie next to Chan. I thought, *Well, maybe now that his dream has come true, he's gotten his horses, he's going to die. He's sleeping and sleeping and he's never going to wake up. This is it. It's over.* I noticed how strange it was that I should feel so sad and afraid, yet so calm at the same time. Such a clear feeling of, *Well, there's nothing I can do. This is just happening. How relaxing.* I supposed this was due to the chronically desperate and urgent state of my mind, always asking myself, *What else can I be doing for him? What about his vitamins? Have I given them all—at the right time? His juice? Time for another? Some food. I need to make him something he likes that's good for him, no salt, no sugar. What? He needs more exercise, more sleep, more play, more friends, more laughter, more cuddling. I need to do more . . . or he'll die.* So really, death sometimes looked like a welcome rest to a mind that was exhausting me with worry.

I walked downstairs in this state of frightened limbo, and I passed the back door where a tiny black-and-white bundle of fur, a kitten, lay mewing on the cement, a shot of its own excrement nearby. It must have slipped out of its mother's mouth as she walked along on the roof.

Oh great, I thought, *now a tiny creature, eyes not yet open, is going to die here in my home because of a careless mother. I don't think I can stand any bad omens today.*

I asked Dtaw if it would die.

"No. Don't you hear its mom calling for it from over the fence? She will come for it when we're out of the way. Cats don't die easily."

I certainly hoped it wouldn't. I kept checking as I passed the window to see if it was still alive.

Late the next afternoon Chan looked up at me as I stood stacking the clean dry plates in the cabinet. "Mom, can we go for a bike ride?"

"Sure, honey, if you feel like it. Where do you want to go?" It was the cooling hour before sunset when going out under the sky became a possibility again after the long hot afternoon.

"I want to ride along the river to where Daddy's friends have goats."

Water buffalo, great big Brahman bulls, pigs, chickens; there was no shortage of livestock on the farms adjacent to the town, but goats were a novelty, something the children had never seen.

"Okay, sweetie. I'll get things ready while you sit with Daddy."

Settling Chan's skinny body onto the cushion tied to the rear rack, I rolled the sturdy old Chinese bike out the gate and into the lane. We rode along the water, Chan's warm hands holding my tummy as he chatted with me. He loved to see the darkening river and the shadows of the jungle on the opposite shore. He especially loved to spot bats flicking through the darkness searching for insects. I could almost never see them before they vanished, but he was an expert. He'd adored bats ever since that day, long before he got sick, when we biked down a wide path through golden rice fields to a cave temple, famous for the half a million bats that flew out of it at dusk each night. Later we often recalled the reticulated python, the world's longest snake, yellow and brown and as big around as my thigh, that appeared out of the broken rice stalks and made its way, liquid solid, across the path just in front of us. Chan stood in the trailer behind watching intently as its twenty-foot-long body and tail disappeared on the other side. Awed and mesmerized by its immense presence so near to us, it didn't occur to me, or him either I think, to feel frightened, only blessed.

At the place where the goats lived, we stopped our bikes and went to the fence. Chan timidly held out his hand, reaching for the thick tangle of rough fur between the bearded animal's eyes. The other goats pressed in, and we petted all of them. Tahn pulled some of the long thick grass stems growing beyond their reach, and held them to the biggest goat's mouth. The goat sniffed and declined. Once they realized we had nothing good to feed them, the animals lost interest and retreated.

We turned away and walked down the steps close to the water. From the woven farmer's bag hanging over my shoulder, I pulled out a small bottle of hand sanitizer, relic of my time as the rule-following mother of a bone-marrow-transplant patient when we'd been indoctrinated in the fear of bacteria lurking everywhere. With Chan's immune system suppressed by medication that we hoped would allow the donor's alien marrow to make itself at home in Chan's body, I had learned extreme vigilance about germs. The boys were used to regular treatments of soapy handwashings and, when a sink wasn't available, alcohol gel before meals. We waved our hands in the air to let the fumes dissipate. Then, from the bag, I pulled out sections of green pumpkin I had boiled before we left, and we ate the wet, sweet treat while the sky grew darker and we talked.

Across the river Chan spotted a tree, towering above the others. Against the gray sky of Laos, Chan showed me how its black shadow looked unmistakably like a rearing stallion, head curved beautifully into its neck. He sat entranced with his discovery.

"Mama, why don't real horses look like in the movies and books? Real horses look kind of dirty and messy."

"The horses in the movies are groomed."

"What is *groomed?*"

"That means they stand still while their trainers comb and brush their coats to make them look glossy and beautiful."

"Oh."

"Our horses are workhorses, not show horses. They wear their coats like their cousins in Mongolia in the wild. Do you think we should groom them?" I hoped that the maternal manipulation of the argument wasn't too obvious.

"No, I like them natural," Chan replied.

Sitting close together in the darkness, talking with my son, I told myself I must remember all the things he said so I could write them down. But when I sat down to do so later, most of his words had vanished. Why does life disappear like water falling through my fingers? I still can't fathom that I can't remember so much of my boys' infancy and early childhood. Where did the recordings of all that happened go in my brain? Are they there or did they somehow never get properly entered? How can something so precious as our lives just disappear when it feels as though it's all that means anything? Why is it trivial things like furniture and clothes can stay and clutter up our space till they, or we, rot, when what matters most is gone in a heartbeat?

On the way home in the dark, Chan suddenly blurted out, pointing up to the moon, "I can see that round part—you know the one that doesn't shine up, the outline—I can see it!" I smiled at his delight and wrongly explained that it's called the dark side of the moon.

"Like in that song from *Mulan*: *mysterious as the dark side of the moon*," I reminded him.

"*Mulan*'s a good movie because it tells you to use your power." His voice carried, quiet but firm from behind me, as we rode home under the purple sky, sidewalk dim in the darkening evening. But I'd ridden this way so many times before. I knew my way.

At home the kitten was gone, and the mother's anguished cries had stopped. Certainly, she had brought it home and it was going to be fine.

PART 5

THE MOUNTAIN

*T*HE DAY WE FINALLY LEFT TO MOVE TO OUR CABIN in the mountains, Jew was visiting from Bangkok. Hurrying her away from her grandmother's protests that the mountains were no place for a girl, I lifted my niece high over the metal tailgate of the Land Rover, depositing her between Cody and Chan.

"Dtaw, hurry. Let's go before your mother changes her mind," I called as my husband climbed up behind the wheel. Soft blankets covered crates of clothing and food that crammed the bed of the Land Rover. The boys and Jew waited, eager for the trip. The day was lovely. The four children lay down on the blanket as we drove, their toes waggling over the tailgate. They were singing and laughing and Chan was a full part of it. A day worth remembering.

When we rolled to a stop in front of our cabin four hours later and Dtaw turned off the engine, the children jumped from their seats and over the sides of the vehicle as if into cool water on a hot day. At last, the earth, the sky, so much of both without overhead wires and sounds of televisions and loudspeakers to interrupt any of it. At last we were where Chan had begged to be throughout his sickness.

We hurried to the front of the cabin where it faced east toward the line of mountains thirty kilometers away, across a valley of fields and mounded hills far below ours. We climbed the five rough steps up to the porch and Cody picked up the broom, a bundle of dry grasses, ends spread by thick string neatly woven between the stems, and began sweeping the dead leaves and gecko droppings, letting them fall through the wide cracks between the floorboards to the dirt below.

Dtaw opened the narrow door, and the rest of us followed him into the square bedroom, barely bigger than the two-inch-thick coconut-husk mattress we'd brought to lay on the floor for the five of us (six as long as Jew stayed) to sleep on. I reached the small window on the other side in half a dozen steps and slid the narrow stick from the holes in the latches, swinging open the two pieces of wood to let in the light. Lifting the children one at a time, we admired the view to the west of closer mountains and the housetops of the village huddled by the stream a mile below.

Then everyone, even two-year-old Tahn, began carrying bedding, towels, pots, and the rest of the supplies from the Land Rover. Cody and Jew climbed onto the rack on top of the canvas roof and set to work on the knots where their bikes were lashed down. Dtaw stood below, directing Jew and Cody which bike to hand him first. Soon the sound of dirt bikes buzzed from the road, and five young boys, agile and energetic, arrived to meet their new friends and help with the move in. When the gear was unloaded, Dtaw set them all to work with Cody and

Jew cutting the sharp grass that never stopped striving up from the dust. With hoe blades, they chopped at the short tufts, giving us a place to play and eat and sit around the fire.

Through all of it, Chan sat at the outdoor table, watching, wishing to help, but at least content to have finally arrived where he for so long dreamed of being. Each time we passed him, he reached out to touch us, or smile, or share a joke.

At dinnertime, Uncle Shoon arrived unexpectedly. He had come up to get Jew before dark and was in a hurry to get back home. It didn't matter that the family had agreed she could spend the night. The mountains are no place for girls, according to Dtaw's mother's generation. There was no arguing with the elders on this.

A few days after we arrived at our cabin, Chan became more weak and listless than usual. We realized he probably needed red blood cells and traveled back down to the hospital in the capital to get them. We settled ourselves into the clean hospital room overlooking fields and hills that spread out from the cluster of white cement buildings that comprised this up-country town. We waited for the results of the blood test and subsequent infusion.

Hours later the blood still waited in its bag hanging from the pole by Chan's bed. "Mama, if this one doesn't work, please don't let them do it again," he turned his tear-stained face up to mine and pleaded.

I couldn't promise anything. There was nothing I could do to soothe him. He had to have the blood, and puncturing his skin and sliding the needle into a vein was the only way for the nurses to get it into him. But after eight tries, they couldn't find a vein that worked. The second nurse said his veins were too delicate because he was dehydrated and feverish. I kept trying to think of another way to get the IV fluid and blood into him without these fruitless and painful pokes. (Surgery? Ingestion?) The answers were impossible, but my brain couldn't stop searching, frantic for a solution.

In four hours, three different nurses leaned over his arm, his wrist, then his leg. Each of them, after the first failed attempts, grimaced in concentration, strands of black hair escaping from under white cap, bobby-pinned in place. None could not get a good path for the blood. When the needle did find a vein, the blood either would not drip in from the bag, or the site would become painful and swollen, evidence of vein leakage. When the ruthless ICU nurse came in, poking his leg three times without hesitation or visible emotion despite his screams, the blood began to drip steadily.

We slept. At two a.m. Chan woke up to pee. As he drifted back to sleep, I looked up at the IV tube and noticed the blood had stopped moving. In a panic, I called the nurse. She figured out that it was because he was sleeping with his leg bent. She gently straightened it so as not to wake him from the bliss of sleep, and the precious liquid began to flow again.

A week later, back at the cabin, Mama Tong arrived perched sidesaddle on the back of Paw Cam's rickety motorbike as it chugged up the last steep part of our hill. Smiling with her contagious enthusiasm, Tong hopped off the motorbike once Cam swung the kickstand down to the dirt and hurried to press today's treasures into our tired hands. Fresh, tender fiddleheads gathered from the edge of the stream below her sprawling garden; wild pennywort, glossy green faces like giant shamrocks, the plant we pressed to make the bitter juice that Chan had learned to swallow, believing what we hoped, that it might beat back the cancer; balls of sweetened sticky rice stuffed with black bean paste and coated with flakes of coconut, all raised and harvested by Tong and Cam from the land they worked and loved. Like the plants they coaxed to keep on this side of life despite blight and drought, we too lived on their land, soaking fortitude from the ground under us. We brightened with their coming, and slowed and folded a little in on ourselves each time they left.

Dtaw was building things every day. Hammering nails and sawing wood and digging holes, leaving me alone with our dying child. I had to leave the house every day to force him to be with Chan and to give myself some rest. *I must get on those horses*, I thought. I knew long rides would be restful. Dtaw and Tong were only too glad when I left. When I wasn't there, Chan stopped crying and enjoyed himself, going for trailer rides, spotting eagles, watching the horses.

One of the mental struggles that went on for me every day was whether or not to talk to Chan about the fact that he could be dying. As much as I tried each day to be positive and hopeful, I did think the evidence pointed to his imminent demise. The way his joints ached, the way his face seemed puffy, his fatigue, and all the hopeless prognoses we'd heard over and over—all combined to make my rational mind unable to release the sense that our days with him would be few. All my education and cultural background told me it was unfair and dishonest not to say, "Well, Chan, this is what leukemia looks like just before people die. There's a good chance you're dying."

But the other theory, which I was starting to see, was that there was just as good a chance that he wasn't yet dying, that perhaps the pain he was experiencing then was the same pain that he would struggle with for months or years until he died, or that he might even miraculously overcome. To put the idea "I am dying" into a person's head is a very powerful thing to do, and I didn't believe, even when he was so sick, that it was fair to do that to Chan. I told myself that when he was getting transfusions once a week and infections regularly and his platelets were not holding up, then maybe we'd talk about it, but not until then, not yet. Of course, my fear was that dying was *his* biggest fear, yet he was afraid to voice it because I was afraid to voice it. How could I address that fear without putting the thought into his head? This circular question worried me every day.

"Honey, I think it's dishonest and unfair not to talk to Chan openly about what's happening to him," I said to Dtaw. The boys were all asleep and Dtaw and I sat up in the kitchen. We were tired but I wanted to talk. Dtaw looked at me and listened quietly, sitting still on the floorboards close to the glow of the fire. "We need to tell him there's no way he can get through this. He has so much cancer it's pouring out of his joints, causing swelling and pain, and he's going to be anemic again soon if he isn't already even though he just got more red cells on Tuesday."

Dtaw remained quiet as usual.

I plowed on as I had gotten used to doing in the face of his silences: "What are we going to do when his platelets get so low we have to fly him to Bangkok for a transfusion or risk his bleeding to death? Are we going to put him through that exhausting trip?"

Before Dtaw had time to formulate a response or hold me close, the familiar whimpering began again in the bedroom, and I got up to check on Chan.

In the dark bedroom he was half-asleep and scared. He must have thought I was Dtaw. *"Nuwat lang"* (massage my back), he said in a small voice. I rubbed the smooth skin that covered the bumps of his bones, hoping in my exhaustion and in my need to talk to my husband that he would soon sleep. When I heard Dtaw snoring in the kitchen, I spoke through the spaces in the wall: "Come to bed."

The next morning, Chan woke up and wanted to get dressed immediately to go down to Tong's house to watch his favorite TV show. While I was gently pulling the loosest pair of pants and shirt over his swollen joints, he said, "If I could just get this ankle better, I could stand up."

What? I hadn't heard him talk that positively in a long time.

Then, rolling down the bumpy road in the trailer, he kept saying things like, "Oooh, I hate being this sick. I just want to get well. I wish there was no pain in the world . . . Mom, six days after I get all well, can we go to that place for special time where we had cereal? I've been wanting to go to that place for a long time." I knew the place he meant, a restaurant in a lush garden of flowers in the middle of a verdant valley an hour down the mountain. It was the last place Chan had played a game of tag with Cody, Tahn, and Jew. And when I was getting organized to go make my phone calls while Chan watched his show, he smiled at me and said, "Have a nice phone call, Mom!"

I couldn't believe it. Maybe not yet.

After I returned from hiding in the tall grass, clutching my cell phone and crying to Maggie as the herdsmen ambled by with their knobby-kneed cattle, wooden bells clacketing with each step, I came home with renewed energy to sit with Chan. He showed me how he could now stretch his arm out straight and how he could straighten both legs and flex his toes and ankles. He also reminded me that he deserved a big reward for getting his line out, a grueling medical procedure; he wanted something from Bangkok, something new he'd never seen before, because, after all, the toys change every year, and oh, he'd need another game card for the Game Boy, but that wouldn't count as the real reward.

TIME

A COOL BREEZE BLEW UP THE STEEP HILLSIDE, causing the sharp blades of grass to sway in the morning sun, a moving fringe underlining the dark green stillness of the valley and waves of blue mountains beyond. A butterfly, papery and backlit yellow, fluttered past the nearest trees while a brittle brown leaf, huge as an elephant's ear, fell from above and crashed heavy on the dry grass below. Two months since the end of the rains, and leaves were finally beginning to yellow and die. The jungle below was not entirely still. Above the tangle of young trees and reaching vines, the huge frayed leaf of a banana tree swayed slightly. Where a branch of feathery bamboo stretched toward the sky, the wind played with it like fingers touching a beloved's hair.

I'd washed Chan's hair the day before, but he was sweating so much at night with a fever that he awoke with it wet and matted again. By the time he cried about the pain in his limbs and how he couldn't go anywhere and how he didn't want to head down to the village with Daddy because he hated to leave me because he didn't get enough time with me when he was little (fresh sobs and tears with every one of these items), his hair had dried fine and soft and sweetly messy.

Cody had his turn to complain when he heard he had to go to the village too and wouldn't get time with me. "But you promised!" he screamed, and threw pillows till it was time to leave. Two-year-old Tahn was pushed aside by me and threatened by Dtaw. Chan sat quietly eating his almonds and raisins in the sunlight that streamed through the doorway of the dark kitchen.

"Actually, Mama," Chan said, looking up and smiling at me when I turned toward him, "I think I'll take a nap after TV so you can rest more."

I kissed his cheek, thankful to see him smile, then I continued to prepare their things so I could shoo them all away. Cody shouted and Dtaw complained. I thought of the day before when I calmly and quietly got all three of them out of the house by six thirty a.m., returning at three thirty p.m., giving Dtaw nine hours of uninterrupted time, and here I had to be screamed at and tortured with tears just to get a couple of hours on my own.

But finally they were gone. Chan let me carry him to the Land Rover parked beyond the outhouse. "I think we can try the huggy carry," he said, without a wince or whimper. At the car, I laid him down across the front seat. Another smile while I kissed him goodbye. Cody even let a smile escape when he dodged my goodbye kisses. "Another five minutes of time with me this afternoon if you kiss me!" he threatened. I waved till the Land Rover bounced out of sight down the dusty road lining the fold between the rice fields, stalks dry and broken on the earth.

Now I could sit and sip my tea and gather myself, at

last feel the churning mud puddle that was my mind absorbing their sobs and needs and hurts and sickness begin to settle and clear to quiet.

I wished I had told Dtaw in no uncertain terms to stay away till one o'clock and to leave Tahn in the village with Cam, so I could play with Cody and Dtaw could sit with Chan. I had left it open-ended. *If he comes back before ten a.m.,* I thought, *I'll kill him.*

My tea was cold. My throat was sore. I went to heat up more. I decided not to wash dishes that morning.

It is a very hard thing we are doing, living with this illness of Chan's, of ours, I thought. He was crying so much. But then that morning when he realized he would be without me for a few hours, he had stopped and smiled. He seemed to have some control over his strong emotions, but it felt to me like he wasn't crying simply for attention. The day before he had called to me and said, sobbing with Daddy, "I just feel like I need to let my feelings out now." At first he cried about having his line taken out, and then about his difficult life.

I felt pulled to want to let him hurry up and die just because I didn't like to see so much sadness. But I knew it wasn't sensible to say, "Well, if things are this bad, better to be dead." I also noticed that when things looked bad, I felt like they would only get worse, which was not always the case. Chan seemed better that day. In the night he had even sat up without my help. I wondered if with all the crying he was working his way toward a fighting stance. He even drank the dreaded apple-celery juice without complaint and ate a whole bowl of yellow split pea soup before they left.

It's not over yet, I told myself.

I stretched back in the one chair we had. The smooth cool slats of wood connected by rope made a swinging bridge suspending my legs and back and bottom just right. With my feet resting on the railing of cut saplings that kept us from tumbling over the edge of the porch and down to the valley below, I thought about how comfortable I was. I had noticed the day before, in the midst of running for something from the bedroom, that I never sat down. This was the third time in as many weeks that I'd sat in that chair and rested.

A few days later I sat cross-legged on the dark boards by the kitchen fire, Chan in my lap, his slender limbs tense with upset, his small fists clenched as he cried. It had been days since I'd had a break from taking care of him, and I was tired. I wondered where processing all that misery would take him. He expended so much energy raging that I never thought of him as frail, no matter how thin he got. When his sobs slowed enough to tell me his fears, I listened as if our lives depended on it.

"I'm just afraid when you go away from me you'll get sick and go in the hospital and never come back," he finally confessed.

"Honey, nothing could keep me away from you. Nothing. Not a hundred strong men, not tigers, not guns. I would always fight my way back to you, no matter how sick I was. And besides, I know how to stay well. I've learned from you how to fight," I reassured him, relieved to finally know what fear was driving this latest upset so I could try to fix it.

Another time he complained he was sick of being ordered around, that there was someone in his heart yelling at him, but he was doing the very best he could. He said he was tired of Cody and Tahn trying to annoy him when he never did anything to bother them. When he was crying hard about this with Cody nearby, Cody said, "Well, you *try* to bother me." And then the rapid-fire dialogue that begins so many sibling discussions.

"No I don't."

"Yes you do."

"When?"

"Like when you said, I got to eat corn and you didn't."

"Well, I wasn't trying to bother you."

"Well, you did."

"Well, you should've told me."

"Okay. I will next time."

And they quieted down again, satisfied.

That afternoon, when I was walking my bike up the steepest part of the road where it turns back toward our hut and the water jars finally come into view between the yellow hill and the blue sky, Chan spoke to me from the plastic seat on the rear rack: "I hated it when we were in Seattle and you and Daddy were cranky and I would go by myself and sit in a corner and cry by the heater."

I listened, amazed that he remembered and disgorged these heartbreaking memories. I kept telling myself, *He's processing his way to health, he's getting rid of what doesn't serve him,* but these tidbits that bubbled up all day long astonished and pained me.

"I hate being here. I hate being like this. I'm so miserable. I just want to have fun. I just want to be happy. I just want to walk."

All his complaining made me constantly second-guess my decisions. *Maybe we're in the wrong place. Maybe he belongs in a city where he can go to malls and museums and movies. Maybe he should be by the river with his friends. Maybe here is nice for me and Dtaw but boring for a sick six-year-old. Maybe he belongs in a hospital where he could just have plenty of morphine and Cartoon Network and entertaining people dropping by and then he could just be quiet and comfortable and die that way. Not be miserable like he is here on a windy mountain.* These thoughts cycled in and out of my consciousness.

Then when I had some time to myself, I was looking at pictures from the previous month, pictures of him with his brothers and the neighbors who came up to visit, pressed in close around him; of him at Cody's soccer game sitting in Tong's lap in a crowd of cheering families; in Cam and Tong's front yard watching the chickens in their endless fidgeting and pecking; sitting with Tong's sister's family palms out and open to the village fire. I realized that he belonged here. He hated hospitals. He shut down in them. They would have given him so much morphine he'd be dead by now, quiet and not miserable and not in pain, but dead.

I knew his crying and misery were just good processing and the right thing for him to do. I knew he'd rather be in the bosom of his family, noisy and raucous and crabby as it was, than lying lonely and lost in a hospital bed. This had to be the right place.

The next morning, I woke up to cold wind and wet wood on the porch. I woke long before it was time to get up as we always went to bed when darkness made it too hard to see snakes or scorpions or stinging bugs where we stepped. I lay on the thin mattress, eager to get a fire blazing, but

Chan had me pinned in his usual leg-and-arm-wrapped-across-my-body grip.

Tahn woke up full of play as usual. "Mama!" he called to me across his daddy's chest, rising and falling gently in sleep. "Shhh..." I smiled back at him. "Don't wake Chan!" He crawled over Dtaw to where I lay, and we cuddled and joked, me shushing him every minute. Finally he started to complain of a tummy ache, which turned into, "I have to poop." I quickly disengaged from Chan's embrace and scurried to find sweaters and hats before braving the cold drizzle.

On the way from outhouse to kitchen, I balanced Tahn's warm body against my hip and leaned over the wood piled against the outside kitchen wall, searching for a dry piece for the breakfast fire. Inside Tahn watched from where he sat next to me, small fingers fluttering against my knee as I lifted the machete from its corner behind the bucket stove and chopped splinters of wood. Chan called out from the bedroom, "Mama! I'm awake!"

"Okay, honey. I'll be there in a little bit. Let me get the fire started."

But he kept calling for me until his calls turned to crying. I kept thinking, *Why doesn't he call for Daddy? He's right there next to him.* I continued to pull last night's dishes from the mouse-proof glass cabinet, set the tray for our breakfast, refusing to respond to Chan's lament.

"Nobody is taking care of me," he cried, until he became so angry he maneuvered himself, crawling on hands and knees, down the three steps from the bedroom to the smaller room beside it. "You'd better hurry up!" he threatened, by now furious. "I'm about to go out the door with no hat or coat!" The love of my life was still sleeping comfortably through all of this, but I was mostly used to that by then. Well, not really. When I finally went to Chan and finished dressing him and asked Dtaw if he was planning to join the morning preparations for school, it took some effort not to kick my husband in the ribs.

I carried Chan through the narrow doorway, the two steps across the porch and down the stairs, around the corner of the hut, and into the side room that was our kitchen. I settled him on the floor, wrapped in a blanket. He watched, quieted by being together.

Once the wood caught, the coals glowed pink at their edges and finally gray enough that I could put the pan over them to warm up last night's stew for breakfast. I laid the dishes and sticky rice basket on the big enamel tray between shooing Tahn out of the kitchen, listening to Chan whine, and rushing Cody along, criticizing his outerwear selection and then later defending him from Dtaw's criticism of the same.

When Dtaw walked stiff and sleepy down the stairs to start the day, I slipped away without a word to check on the horses. Dew on broken grass wetting my toes, I let gravity pull me gently down the hill to their warm forms moving on the land. Their coats were soaked with mist, but Dap was the only one shivering. With a length of stout tree branch on the ground nearby, I knocked the wooden stake from side to side, loosening it from the ground where it held his tether in place. Dap turned from me and immediately began walking purposefully up the hill toward the taller grass. I leaned my back against air, pulling on the lead line that trailed out behind him and calling, *"Yu! Yu!"* (Stay! Stay!) as he dragged me, skidding like a water-skier in slippery flip-flops through the mud, rice stalks, and manure piles. Finally he slowed down at the tall grass.

I pounded the anger of my bruised ego into the ground with the stake and went down the hill to bring Tolay up too. He had pulled his stake from the ground in the night and gone below to the banana trees to strip the huge leaves from their stems. His line was wrapped up in the mess of vegetation, so I set to work untangling it and led him up to Dap. Tolay was much better behaved. He always let me believe I was leading him rather than the other way around. After unwinding the other three horses' ropes from the stump they were tied to, I trudged back through the wind and rain to untangle whatever mess was brewing in the kitchen.

After breakfast, Dtaw, Cody, and Tahn set off through the mud to walk Cody to school. Chan settled into his usual narration of woes as I cut the vegetables for his juice. He renewed his most recent claim that he would no longer eat unless it was tuna fish sandwiches purchased and consumed at one of the two acceptable restaurants located in or near the resort town, an hour drive down off the mountain and toward civilization. I listened, begging him to change his mind and eat good food, with the aim of eliciting more anger and indignation, which seemed to do him good. He refused and fought and screamed and cried until I had finished preparing and boiling the fresh greens Tong had gathered for him from her garden the day before. He ate half the plate without complaint before gagging so that I let him stop.

The next morning, I watched with quiet wonder again as the world turned toward the east. The returning sun crested blue-black mountains, green leaves turned gold, birds sang from every side, wood bores buzzed, and clothes drying on the line fluttered softly. Behind me, the fire I'd made when the sun was only a promise had burned down to embers.

Earlier I had awakened to find the hard dirt bathed in blue-white light from the full moon. In bright moonlight— no need for a flashlight—I gathered wood and splintered kindling and lit the breakfast fire.

Then cutting the apple and celery for Chan's juice, fighting with Tahn for turns with the knife, then fresh rice to the pot, then embers settled, just right to cook without burning. The sky lightened to soft purples with smoky black clouds wandering over the mountain, the fog on the valley floor thinning almost visibly as the sun advanced. Chan called to me, *"Buwat kee!"* (I have to poop). I carried him outside and to the steep slope below the hut. There I crouched with Chan over the new hole Dtaw had dug in the black soil. Chan, naked from the waist down, sat suspended between my legs so he could be comfortable while he pooped, my hands wrapping nearly all the way around his bird-leg thighs. More bird songs filled the air and the spreading light became harder on the eyes but warmer on the skin, almost undoing the cool of the breeze. The full moon paled into the brisk morning blue, comforting as a covenant that the world would again turn to quiet night after another hard day.

So often when I felt overwhelmed with living with the fear of grief from Chan's probably imminent death, I looked around. And being there with the trees and mountains and sky and sun, I was assured that everything would be okay. Whatever happened to Chan, the trees would keep blossoming, the birds nesting, the moon shining. Somehow I felt certain that life would continue and be okay. I wondered if living elsewhere I could be thus calmed. Green humps, a line of hills far below, floated like islands in a cloud. The shadows of the trees that grew from them cut long straight lines slanting toward me through the sunlit mist.

And then blue, blue, blue. Everything blueing up. Bright between the leaves, the sun burnished the wide blades of grass and the soft coats of the gentle horses standing in the field.

Laundry, stuffy bedding, breakfast waited. This morning I would not rush. *The sun does not rush. The birds and horses do not. I will sit here with the living creatures a bit longer,* I thought, *no movement to the next task yet.*

The day before I'd taken the boys down to the village to watch television at Tong's house. We were busy with juice and baths and shampoo and medicines and taking walks. Dtaw spent the day at home raking up dead grass, hoeing steps into the dirt, tidying up the land. When we returned, the bed was still unmade.

At nine o'clock the next morning, the sun shone too bright in my eyes for me to see the computer's screen, but I liked that. I could just sit and soak in the morning UV rays and let my fingers fly. That morning while I swept the dust from the kitchen floor and then sprinkled the water from washing the vegetables over the floorboards before rubbing the tattered old rag of a wool sweater over them, I asked myself why, knowing that the computer is waiting on the porch and the children are down the mountain, why did I feel compelled to keep a journal? Why did I want to record the little meaningless details of our life here?

I did it because I wanted to hold on to that time, that time before Chan died, or the time he was getting well, the time we were just living day to day with one clear purpose: to care for Chan, to help his body heal or ready him for death, I didn't know which one.

Our lives seemed very beautiful then. There was the beauty of the physical world around us, but it was more than that. Everything was stripped bare. All that we cared about was being with our children, working hard toward wellness and some sort of understanding. Every day I marveled at Tahn's stout tan body, his cherry-red lips and white teeth, and at Cody's growing muscular, agile frame. Because I was holding a small, crying skeleton of a boy all day, the healthy, happy boys were a double delight to me, if not to Chan, who cried when he watched little Tahn run joyfully as fast as his thick legs could carry him. And in some terrible way, they offered me a kind of assurance. *Well, if Chan dies, I will be left with these very healthy boys.* I hated it when I had thoughts like that. I could not imagine the horrible hole that would be left in all our lives if Chan died. But things did seem to be headed in that direction—the swollen joints, the pain, the discomfort, the way food didn't taste good, lips pale again only two weeks after his last transfusion, and that was when we transfused when his hematocrit was above twenty, just as a cushion. But I told myself not to get sunk into that fear, to instead keep fighting for him every day, every step.

His crying was getting predictable. He was so miserable, I was so mean, he felt so bad, he would say, and the tears would flow. But I told myself crying was the right thing for him. Two days before he'd screamed at me and even Dtaw. He looked into my eyes while he was screaming and asked furiously, "How would YOU like to be ME?"

But after a nap, he was much more content. And the day after that, he really seemed to enjoy himself. When several young children were playing in Tong's kitchen and I placed him down in the doorway while I finished putting away the dishes, he even sat and didn't ask to be taken out of sight of their staring. He told me later that he felt better in the mountains than he did in Bangkok because he worried less.

Every morning we went down before breakfast to say hello to the horses. They were so placid. It soothed us. And there was the excitement of the relationship between the three adult males. When they squared off and rippled their muscles and nipped and gathered together and parted, it was impossible to look away. I wanted to figure out how they could roam free not tethered to their stakes.

Grateful for the sight of distant peaks, sometimes hidden in a haze, sometimes dark silhouettes against the blue, edges cut clean by the rising sun, I could see three ranges in three directions: east, south, and west. To the north, our cabin sat beside a path winding up into the darkness of the jungle.

But the mountains and valley and sky might always be like this. My family would not. My family ran and tumbled and tangled and cried and changed by the millisecond.

The day before, in search of good cell phone reception, I'd found a secluded hilltop in the middle of acres of dry fields, miles from the village. I had just crouched down on the earth to confide my miseries into the ear of my friend at the other end of the call, when Cody and his gang emerged over the crest of the hill like a band of ragged elves, cheeks cracked and tan, eyes shy and bright at seeing me. Who could be sad after that? Cody was roaming free, getting tall and strong and slightly arrogant. His sweetness was covered a little by the boyish roughness, but it was still there. I found it one day when I was typing at Tong's house and he came in for his afternoon bath. He hadn't expected to see me and came over and rested his head on my knee to watch me work, trying to pick out English words that he knew on the screen.

Dtaw remained steadfast and hardworking. He continued to hold out endless hope for Chan's recovery when mine was gone. He was never dramatic or loud. I cried about Chan's dying and he only looked at me each time and said, "He will get well."

I cried about not knowing if we were in the right place for Chan. When I worried about this aloud with Dtaw, he would look at me and say, "We are here for only one purpose: to get Chan well."

Dtaw worked hard on the cabin and the earth around it, raking and cutting and planting and building. He took the boys on horseback rides. He talked about what we would plant in the spring. He held his back and groaned. He fell on the ground whenever he sneezed, as if dodging a grenade, to decrease the pressure the sneeze put on his ruptured disc. But he kept going every day. He never complained. He listened to Chan rant and sob. He held firm when Chan begged to be taken out or not drink his juice or not eat his brown rice.

Chan was working hard too. Sometimes I wished he would die so he wouldn't have to work so hard, so he wouldn't have to eat food he didn't like, so he wouldn't have to feel pain. But then I knew that was absurd. Life is simply very hard sometimes, but you never give up. People survive concentration camps, war, rape, starvation. You just don't give up.

And then there was me. *How are you?* people would ask. *Fine.* I was. Sometimes I was so happy, usually when no one else was around grabbing for my attention. And sometimes I was so tired of being heartbroken, like when Chan told me he wished I wouldn't be so crabby all the time and when he wept about how awful it was the night he was crying in pain and I got up and moved away from him. It was when I couldn't take another hour of it, so I made room, woke Dtaw up, and demanded that he take over.

I loved the bare bones of our life. I loved our table where we ate, slice of tree resting on smaller tree-trunk legs planted deep in the dirt, our simple mattress where we slept, our clothes all in two crates (one for the boys, one for us), our tattered jeans and jackets hanging on nails. I loved making the fire in the morning. I loved washing out my underwear in the dented washtub under the big tree every evening after my bath.

When it rained, it was different. It was muddy and mucky and the bedding and all our clothes got damp. But I thought we could work that out before the monsoons.

In bed the next night, Cody whispered to me a wonderful report of his day at a school soccer tournament. "I got ten different kinds of candy, three oranges, and five jicama!" He was so happy with his treasure trove. I loved to be reminded that he was still just a little boy, though with all the help he was to us, I often thought of him as my equal. I wondered how to talk to him about Chan. I thought that if Chan was dying, Cody should know and be able to decide how to work with it.

The next day as we walked home from the village after school, I told Cody, "You know, honey, your friends are coming tomorrow to cheer up Chan, not just to play with you. Chan needs a lot of support right now. He's fighting something that most people die from. You know that, right?"

"Yeah, I know." And then after a few minutes of quiet walking, "But Mom, we can still run around and play while he's sleeping or having a cry, can't we?"

I said yes and told him that if he ever wanted to ask me anything about Chan's illness, he should. After some more silence while we trudged along the dirt road over the mountain, far enough behind Chan, Tahn, Tong, and her two-year-old son Tao to be out of earshot, he said, "I just wish he'd get over the leukemia. I don't care about his legs, but the leukemia I wish would go away."

Earlier that day when Dtaw and I escaped our parenting duties for forty-five minutes while the boys were occupied at Cam and Tong's with their favorite TV show, I had confessed my worst fears. We had ridden Cam's dirt bike over the rough road to a spot high above the village where we could look down between tall leafy trees, full of birdsong and sunlight, to the two dozen rusty rooftops of the village below. Across the valley on the far eastern ridge, we could just make out the tiny square and triangle that were our house and teepee. We sat talking, Dtaw's thick leather jacket protecting us from the roots and underbrush, and I told him my fear that Chan's death was near.

He thought for a few moments before speaking. "Still eating. Still pooping. I don't think that's what a dying person is like."

I considered his statement. I had to admit Chan still had a healthy appetite, and I supposed if someone were really going to die, he would probably exist without food for at least a week or two first. I laughed quietly at the reality he used to make his point in the face of my insistent pessimism.

"I'm going to die soon! I know I am!"

We were sitting in Tong's living room about to have lunch, and Chan was crying about his pain.

"No, no," I replied quickly, "not when you're doing all this fighting, drinking your juices, eating all this good food, using your power. That's not what a dying person does!"

"Well I'd rather die than be in this pain!"

I murmured that I understood and Dtaw explained that the pain always gets worse just before you get well, just like when you poop.

"Can Daddy just shut up! I am so sick of his explaining this to me. He thinks he's so great!"

More screaming as Tong served lunch and I called Cody in, just down from the mountain with his friends. He said he wasn't hungry, but I made him come in to avoid midafternoon grazing. Dtaw and I dug into the green papaya and fiddlehead salads and hot and sour soup, pungent from the galingale Tong dug from behind the house just before she cooked it, thick with oily Mekong fish we kept in her freezer. Chan screamed louder: "I can't take this anymore! Give me morphine! I need morphine!"

I began to think we should stop eating and hurry up the mountain to get it for him, but I tried to ride it out. The lunch was too good to interrupt.

Finally he asked through his tears, "How can I relax?"

"You don't have to now, if you don't want to," I said, in case he wanted to keep working. Then I realized maybe he knew what he needed, so I added, "Or I can help you." I put down my spoon and began rubbing his back as I spoke soothing words: "Imagine the sky full of fluffy white clouds. You are one of those clouds, soft and gentle and quiet. You float high above the earth, above green rolling hills and . . ."

He settled down. His furrowed brow softened. His hands still rubbed his foot, but even his rapid breathing slowed a little.

I kept talking: "Now you float over a wide beach, silver sand, smooth and clear . . ." I signaled Dtaw to stop scraping his plate and slurping loudly. I feared the resurgence of screaming and crying, refocusing attention on the pain, but Chan rested on and finally, finally his hands stopped rubbing his foot and he drifted off to sleep.

When I tried to wrap up the imagery so I could get back to the tender moist bits of fish in my rice, his eyelids fluttered. I kept on: "And as you float along, other fluffy white clouds join you. You float together through the night, the silvery bright moon and all the many stars keeping watch over you. And as you sleep and dream, you hear a voice, no louder than the beating of your heart, rhythmic as your breathing, saying softly, *May I be well.* *May I be well.* With every breath it repeats, *May I be well,* and then, *May I be happy. May I be free from suffering. May I be at peace.* You hear these words again and again, gentle but strong, every time you return to this quiet place. *May I be well.*"

Chan continued to sleep, and I was amazed yet again that his pain could be so intense, yet he could pass through it and sleep peacefully without the drugs. I had been giving him morphine at night, but that morning he had difficulty peeing, so I was pleased to have been able to put off a dose, if only for a few hours.

Through the open window, I could see Tahn playing happily in the dirt outside, kicking a ragged soccer ball with Tong. All morning he played at the neighbors' houses, sharing the children's food and sweets. He was so happy to have people around him all the time. Cody loved being with his friends too. When we came down to the village, I rarely saw the two of them, so busy were they with their comrades. If only Chan could have enjoyed the same fun.

~~~

HORSES

~~~

THE HORSES SOOTHED US. They spoke in grunts and breath and nickers. They expressed what they wanted to say with shudders of flesh, movement of ears, and sidesteps of heavy honest hooves. Each day we went out to squat near them just to listen, to watch. Sometimes we held out strands of yellow grass, hoping they'd walk, in their casual way, over to lip up the bristly snack. Sometimes we took cold sticky rice with us from the house and pull fistfuls from the basket, holding it out in our open palms until they came to take the treat.

Chan would peer up from the trailer, fine brown hair ruffled by the breeze, smiling at the softness of their warm breath, the tickle of the stiff whiskers of their noses. "You know what's even better than your kisses, Mama?"

"What, honey?"

"Horse lips."

I was glad to see him happy.

And in the afternoons, when Dtaw had finished working, he lifted the leather saddle from where it hung over the porch railing and walked down to the pasture where the horses grazed. He set it on the rail of the corral, and led the least aggressive stallion from the field inside the small circle of fence to saddle up and ride.

The horses were not used to saddles, and Dtaw was not used to horses. But he was determined, and I've never known a man with more confidence. So after he rode for a little, to test out Tolay's mood, he would lift Cody, because he was the biggest and most physically re-silient of the boys, up onto the horse's back, holding the halter short and firm in his fist in case Tolay bucked. And with the same quiet power that we all trusted, Dtaw led the horse around the ring, satisfied at last to be able to give his children what they wanted.

He wanted Chan to ride too. I watched, frightened of what a hard fall from such a height might do to such a fragile body, noting the way the size of the animal made Chan's legs seem even thinner, little more than bones and skin by now. But Chan smiled, enjoying what he'd dreamed of for so long, feeling the animal walk rhythmic and solid beneath him, smelling the warmth of its strong body, holding him up.

Chan's feet and hands were swollen where the toes started like the white rubber infant doll I'd had as a little girl. Her heavily lashed blue eyes closed lazily when I laid her down, and her feet and hands had that same weird bulge of fat, only Chan's was more exaggerated and more grotesque. One morning he looked at me and quite calmly said, "I think when it's swollen that means it's leukemia cells."

"You think so?" I replied, trying to assume a light tone of interest. "Like as opposed to toxins?"

"Yeah."

"Is that a good thing?"

"Yeah."

He cried and moaned. But every day he wanted to get up and even eat a little. One day while Dtaw and I sat with him outside, he complained, "I just can't get comfortable! There's nowhere for me to get comfortable! There's nowhere for me to go to have fun! There's nowhere for me to get well!" And he broke into sobs. Then he turned to me and said, "It just feels like I'm going to have cancer for the rest of my life. Do you know how that feels?"

He looked at me as if to ask if I could imagine anything worse.

Well, yes, actually, there's a much worse scenario—that the rest of your life will be only a few weeks long, I thought.

"I'm not going to have it the rest of my life, am I, Mom? Am I?"

"No, no, of course not," I lied, and put my arm around his thin shoulders.

I thought I should tell him there was a good chance this was death by leukemia, and that there was also a possibility that he would heal. But Dtaw kept saying that if he's still eating and still pooping, he's not dying.

When I told the nurse in Bangkok he was in so much pain and thin and his feet and hands were swollen, she asked if he was still eating.

"Yes."

"Oh, well, that's a good sign. The swelling is just part of his disease."

What the hell does that mean? I asked myself. *How long can we go on like this?*

~~~

CLOSER

~~~

*T*HE WHEELS OF THE TRAILER ROLLED OVER the bumps of dead grass and ruts in the road. Chan weighed so little now, only thirty pounds of skin and bone, that there wasn't much work to roll him out to where the horses stood. The late-afternoon sun poured bright on the land. So exposed up there. No hiding from what nature offered. We lived on a wide-open landscape, but up so high above the valley we were never hot. The only shade we needed when the bright sun became too much, we could find under the dry grass of the porch roof or the dark cool of the kitchen with its floor of earth and wood. But that day the sun was already halfway down to the horizon, and the air was cooling.

"Don't go too fast, Mama. You don't want to scare them." Sticky rice basket beside him on the nylon seat of the bike-trailer-turned-wheelchair, Chan was eager to touch Payanak, the colt. So young, he always stayed close to his mother. And though he stretched his neck out toward us in curiosity sometimes when we approached, he always moved in close to her dusty flank before we could pet him.

"He's old enough now," Dtaw had told us that afternoon. "Take him some sticky rice and try feeding him."

I pushed Chan toward where the horses stood a few hundred feet from the hut, heads down, browsing the hard grass for soft shoots. While I pulled the lever that pressed the rubber brake against the tire, Chan turned to open the basket of rice. Lifting up the sticky grains, he rolled them into a ball so that Payanak would be able to take it easily from his small hand. I came around and squatted beside him, watching, waiting. The stems of dead grass pricked my arms and thighs, but I'd long since learned to accept that.

Soon Doc Mai, seeing Chan's outstretched arm, stepped over to us. Her velvety lips and thick teeth moved briefly over his palm, held flat to keep his fingers safe just as I had shown him the day the horses first arrived. Then the ball of rice was gone. From behind her, Payanak peered out at his mother's movements. With tentative steps, he walked forward. With two backward steps for every three forward, he made his way to where Chan waited. I quickly placed another rice ball on Chan's palm. We did not speak, only watched, listening to the whoosh of the breeze in the distant treetops, feeling the warmth of the sun before it vanished. As I watched Chan's face, I saw an expression of serenity and took a moment to soak it in. He looked to me as if there were nowhere else he'd rather be, coaxing the young horse, his face radiating affection and peace. I held still. At last Payanak was close enough, eyeing his mother to be sure this was permitted, and then quickly, in case it wasn't, he stretched out his neck, head turned sideways, to lip up the rice from Chan's palm. Immediately the young horse stepped back to the shelter of his mother's side and chewed the sweet morsel.

Chan turned to me, beaming with the thrill of connection to the young animal. "Did you see that, Mama?"

"Yes, baby."

He began rolling another ball for Doc Mai, who stood closer now, waiting. After both horses had eaten more rice, Payanak stood so close to the trailer, head almost touching Chan's, that Chan carefully reached out to rub the stiff hair that grew above the colt's nose. Payanak stood still as Chan moved his fingers over the flat cowlick in the center of the white patch on his brow. At last the rice was gone and the mother and son moved back to searching for shoots of grass, but not before Chan had time to bathe in the pleasure of their quiet company. I pushed Chan's trailer back to the cabin, both of us silent.

Sometimes when I was worrying, fearing the worst, wondering how I would survive if Chan died, I looked out from the cabin, and there were the horses. Young and old together, quiet in the field, looking so calm and accepting, that it seemed to me they were resting even when they walked. And the way they stayed near one another calmed me. None ever strayed far from the others. Like our family, they seemed contented by being close.

~~~

RELIVING

~~~

"**M**OM! COME HERE! IT'S THAT FEELING. I feel like someone is cutting me up, cutting me open! Mom!"

As Chan screamed and cried in our bed, I asked, trying to calm him, "What are they using to cut you up?"

"Scissors!"

"And what part of you are they cutting?"

Without hesitation he answered, "My chest!"

As I made my way across the bed and over Dtaw to kneel on all fours above my crying child, he clutched at his chest. "It hurts! It hurts!" he screamed.

"It happened a long time ago. There's nothing happening now. You're right here with Mama and Daddy in bed. There's no blood."

"It hurts! Someone is putting a tube in me and it's banging into things." Renewed sobs.

Though I had always worried that one experiences pain despite the use of anesthesia, I had been skeptical. Now I was sure I was hearing Chan describe the operation he had at the beginning of his treatment when a line was inserted into the large vein emerging from his heart.

The doctors wanted him to have a conduit for the highly toxic chemo drugs to enter his bloodstream.

I was intrigued that he used the word *tube* instead of *line* because for the nine months that he had the line, that was the only way we referred to it: *Time to clean your line. You're pulling my line! Watch out for his line! Shall we tape your line again?* It became all but a part of him. So the fact that he said *tube* made it seem like he was using the word to describe something new and alien, confirming my sense that the flood of emotion that was overcoming him that night was memory recorded then and verbalized in exactly the same words as he would have experienced the surgery.

I continued to soothe, "I'm so glad you're getting this out of your system. You don't need to carry this around anymore."

After a bit, he settled down and closed his eyes. I pressed him to talk to me more about this painful experience, but he opened his eyes, looked at me with his very adult rational stare, and said, "I'm going to sleep now, Mom. I promise I'll talk to you about it more tomorrow."

The next night he said to me as he was tossing and turning and feeling that he would never be able to get comfortable, "Oh, I just feel in my body like I'm dead already. Like my eyes are like this," and he rolled his eyes up into his head. "Like I can't feel my skin at all."

At first I was alarmed that maybe he was sensing his own signals from his body, but then I thought about how lately he'd been doing a lot of emotional work on previous hurts, particularly about having his line put in. I thought about how being anesthetized might feel very much like dying. I wondered if his saying, "I feel like I'm already dead," might be another feeling he was trying to process.

The next night after another day of Chan's crying and complaining and my feeling hopeless and him having taken more morphine, we got into bed at six o'clock because Chan wanted to hurry up and lie down and not have to move anymore and not have to deal with anything, just cuddle up with me and go to sleep. He couldn't sleep, however, and kept moaning with misery and sitting up and lying down and begging me to straighten his legs and rub his back and rub the taut strings that his muscles along his thigh bones had become. I did as he begged me, though after hours it seemed to be getting pointless. Finally, at nine p.m., I'd reached my limit.

"Dtaw," I said to wake my husband from his slumber, "I've been doing this for three hours straight every ten minutes. I can't stand it anymore. You've got to take over. I've got to take care of myself." He grumbled something about my attitude and I said, "What? What was that? Did you have something to say to me?" No reply. I crawled to the other side of him and finally dozed a little.

A few minutes later I heard Chan asking for me.

"She's right here," Dtaw was reassuring him.

"I want Mama!"

"I'm right here, honey, I just need a little sleep, Daddy can take care of you."

"Paw! I feel like there's someone with a knife and they're cutting me open and blood is everywhere!" he told his father, his voice panicky. "It hurts. It hurts."

I crawled back over Tahn to be with Chan.

"Ugh. I hate this feeling! It feels like my hands are being cut off and they're bleeding, and my eyes are being cut and they're bleeding. Ugh!" he continued in a panicky terrified voice. "There was my voice, faint, that was my spirit."

I marveled, I didn't even know he knew the word faint. He seemed to be reliving the operation again and talking about his spirit leaving his body.

"Ouch, it hurts! It hurts!" He was trying to raise his head off the pillow (which he hadn't done by himself for days) to point his face toward his chest. "I want to kiss it! I want to kiss it!" he cried desperately.

"Here, I'll kiss it for you, honey," and I did, leaning my face down to kiss the scar above his left nipple where the line had emerged.

"I'm dying! I'm dying while they're putting in my line!"

I kept reassuring him that he was very much alive and lying in bed with us. After a few minutes, he fell asleep.

Chan slept well that night, and did not ask for any morphine the next day. When he slept badly the next night, waking up groaning more than every hour, Dtaw and I agreed to give him morphine.

"No, no, not yet. It's not pain. It's definitely not pain," Chan said. "It's just, I don't know, a yucky feeling."

We followed his lead and did not give him the medicine. He slept well. I thought about how I'd heard that what we perceive as pain is largely fear. Perhaps by releasing that experience of total anesthesia and surgery, a layer of fear was removed, and so his pain was lessened. Perhaps.

STAYING

W ATCHING MY CHILD SUFFER might have been hard, but what threatened to drive me mad was the roller-coaster of my mind reacting to the day-to-day changes in his pain and moods. My thoughts swung wildly between hope that he might get well and near panic that he might not. To live with this mind of mine, I fell back on the practice I had begun when I first got to know Dtaw and first learned about Buddhism. Aiming to keep my mind on the tasks at hand had become a practice for me by the time Chan got sick. I had practiced far less than I would have liked, but even so, this value was a strong part of my belief system.

The large tree stump that beckoned me to sit still and admire the valley that first day we saw this piece of land had long since been chopped down for firewood. In the place where it once stood, the grassy outcropping had been overgrown with slender trees and winding vines.

One morning, Dtaw led me down from the cabin to where the village men had helped him build the fence for the horses so that they could walk untethered over the ground. We turned left at the pasture, away from the waiting horses and into the dense growth that now almost hid the path to the cliff's edge. I was amazed when a few feet into the tangle of limbs and leaves, I saw the ground cleared, and a large wooden platform where the earth fell away. Dtaw led me up onto the square floor of planks nailed tight to the supporting logs below and walked me to the center of it. He turned me toward him, putting his hands on my hips and smiling the smile that melted my heart even then when his hair had become peppered with gray and the flesh around his eyes swollen with fatigue. Those eyes still sparkled with pleasure, as he said, "For you." I looked around at the square of symmetry beneath our feet, a patch of order in the wild around us, and felt the pleasure of his generous gift. With the help of the village men, he had built this floor above the paths of snakes and stinging bugs. He wanted me to have a place where I could sit and calm my mind each morning before I began the work of caring for Chan. As I had done years before when he showed me the cabin, I could only smile and thank him, wishing words were not so inadequate.

I had been snatching spare moments to sit cross-legged on the porch or the bench behind the house or hidden in the dark kitchen to try to let the tired mess of my mind settle into calm whenever I could, but now I had a place to go, to escape, for a little while, the children's constant clamor for attention and Chan's struggle. Here I could sit and let my gaze rest on the valley floor miles below or the misty horizon as the sun climbed over it and try to practice what I believed to be the path through and out of suffering.

Now, each morning, I went to this place, my sacred spot, the place that first drew us here, and I settled my body into the position that had become natural to me, sitting bottom to floor, legs crossed, feet resting on thighs. As I began to listen with all my senses, I felt the breezes play over my skin, heard the whine of insects around me, and sensed the light of the morning filtering into my body. I began to slow down enough to watch my thoughts arise and pass away. I reminded myself of the futility of thinking of the future and of the past. I told myself there is no reality but now. And I tried to bring all of my attention to only the immediate experience of my breathing body. I sat long enough to explore the effort of staying still, working with the habit of effort, trying to ease back on the trying. Doing the work of doing nothing. I sat long enough to let my breath calm my body and counteract the effects of the daily accumulation of fear in my mind.

When I was ready to end my sitting, I always turned to a *metta*, loving kindness, practice. I knew that I needed to cultivate as much self-compassion as I could in those precious moments of quiet before I returned to the exhausting work of mothering. I focused my attention on my heart, feeling its energy warm and strengthen as I silently, with each inhalation, repeated the words that had surprised me when I learned them at the first meditation retreat I sat at a decade earlier: *May I be well.* And after a while, *May I be happy.* And finally, *May I be at peace.* And then, as I felt the glowing energy in my heart generated by these words, I gathered it up to share. Gazing out over the valley, it was easy to imagine *all beings to the east of me* as I wished them wellness, happiness, and peace. Addressing each point of the compass, then ahead, beside, behind, and beneath me, I imagined the slithering, crawling, running, flying creatures of the earth. And I could imagine the people, busy in the villages below or in the cities and towns beyond the mountains, across the continents and oceans, as I wished them all well. As I thought of so many people in so many different nations and places of peace and war, quiet and turmoil, I was reminded that I was not alone in my suffering; that, in fact, this struggle I was engaged in was ordinary, that people all over the world were like me, wanting only well-being and happiness, becoming frustrated by what stood in their way of that.

With this knowledge that I was part of the community of humanity and that I must not waste my time with imagined future scenes of what might happen to Chan, that I must only put my mind fully on the present, I was able to return to the roller-coaster of our fight. And I would rise from my seat, uncramping and stretching my legs, thank the earth for holding me gently, and climb back up the hill to our life.

QUIET

CHAN LAY QUIETLY IN THE SUNNY HAMMOCK, a sleeping bag slung over the pole overhead to block the sunlight from his face. I had tried to reduce the swelling in his wrist by tying one end of my good black silk scarf around his wrist and the other end over the pole above. The valley below dipped a bowl of green from the blue sky.

"Mama, I can't bend my fingers into a fist. Is that okay?" he asked me, desperate.

I assured him he would be able to make a fist again as soon as the swelling went down. Dtaw pressed hot herbal compresses onto his foot and lulled him with soothing words.

The next morning when Chan woke up, he wanted to get dressed and go to the kitchen. He sat alert, watching me and the other children cook. He wanted to go eat at the table outside. And when the children all went to join Dtaw in the Land Rover for a trip up the mountain, he wanted to go too. As we left, he said to me, "This is kind of fun, going somewhere all together."

Unbelievable. He said something was fun.

On the way down, he laid his head against Dtaw's leg and asked to nap. After we got home, he stayed asleep in the front of the parked Land Rover long enough for me and Dtaw to fight and hug and cry and then for me to cook a forbidden fried egg and eat it quickly before he awoke. When he did, I took him down to the hammock, squirted Betadine in his ears and slathered calendula on his nose scab, and we settled down with Harry Potter, a good distraction.

Chan was more subdued and docile in those few days, no more screaming and blaming me. I was relieved over this, but felt guilty because of my relief. When he was angry and loud and screaming, I could see him strong and fighting. When he was quiet and withdrawn, I worried, afraid it was evidence of more and more cancer cells in his brain. It was so hard to know if I should fight for him, reach for him, or let him rest quietly. And then I quickly saw the answer: he would have plenty of time to rest when he died.

It was hard for me to let him fight so much. I desperately wanted to give up, play the passive, miserable, martyred mother of a cancer patient, but I knew that wouldn't have been fair to Chan. The only way was to let him fight for his right to live, no matter how hard it became for me to stay hopeful. When I wanted to give up, I would trudge up the path to the top of the hill where I could cry into the phone with Maggie. She would tell me gently, "Not yet, not yet. Chan still wants to fight." And I could go back in for a few more rounds.

I'd never liked the medical world's war jargon for cancer. *Battling cancer. The war against cancer. The white cell soldiers.* All this was offensive to me until I became the mother of a boy with cancer, and then very little else seemed to fit, not so much for what was going on in Chan's body, but for what was going on with me. Each day I felt I had to rise and ready myself as a warrior. I had to steel myself for another day of staying hopeful and cheerful. It was a battle because I was never allowed to give up. Like a soldier, no matter how hard things got, I had to keep going and summon something from a well of maturity I didn't know I had. I had to learn to act with honor and bravery, no matter how I felt, in order to rise day after day to fight for Chan.

Chan and I spent the morning at Mei Tong's after biking with Cody to school. When I picked him up to carry him to the bike so we could ride home, he winced and cried out in pain. I begged him to say what it was I was hurting, so I could try to fix it. I started crying, "I can't stand to hurt you. I hate to see you hurt."

He immediately stopped. As I strapped him into the bike seat, tears still streaming down my face, he almost smiled at me. He kept saying, "Actually, it doesn't really hurt."

"Does *this* hurt?" I asked with each piece of clothing I tied around his legs to keep them from banging against the seat.

"No. Nothing hurts," he replied without grimacing, without seeming to cover anything up. It was as if he had switched to a part of his brain where he did not need to struggle with the pain. As we biked up the hill, me getting off when it became too steep so I could push the bike, he was quiet but not withdrawn. Suddenly he said, "It's good to have a mom who knows how to cry because then her kids learn how to cry."

I felt gratification swell around my heart, but I fished for more: "And that's good?"

"Yeah, because then the kids can get all their feelings out. And it's good to have kids when you're young, because then you can get a lot of crying done early and then have a lot of fun." He continued in this contented, reflective mood all the way home.

I took advantage of his mood to do some thinking out loud. "You know what I think would work well for me, honey?"

"What?"

"Well, I'm thinking that when you want a cry, if you could say to me, *Mom, how about giving me some attention?* that would help me a lot.

He was agreeable and we went over the angles and advantages. As I pushed the bike along the sunny, dusty road, weaving around rocks and gullies, we talked about how this would make me a better listener, and he brought up the fact that I could also go and have more cries and do more writing too.

"Like this, Mom, like pretend I said, *Mom, can I have some attention?* and you could say, *Well, how about if I go and write for a half . . . a half . . .*" He struggled to come up with the right way to say the time in English. *"An hour and a half first, and you could play with Cody if you want, just remind me,* and then you could write and then come back and play with me and Jew and Cody, right?"

"Exactly!"

He pondered this more. "But sometimes I don't always have to ask, like if I really need to cry, I just cry, right? Because it's always good to cry, right?"

"Oh, absolutely, if you're really right in there, ready to

cry, just go ahead, I'm just thinking of those times when you would be okay if you didn't."

I climbed back on the bike to ride over the curve hugging the edge of the last hill before the steep one that led to our house.

"Chan, when I listen to your sadness and pain and hopelessness all the time, and never see anything else, I get scared that you're not going to get well, which I know is stupid, because you're just showing feelings, but when I was little I was not allowed to do that much, so now I'm a little dense on this subject."

He nodded his understanding. As we rode and talked, he was so rational and cheerful and intelligent. I thought, *Well, I guess he is going to get well after all.* What ridiculous logic.

When we finally got to the long steep road, barely discernible among the rocks and tufts of grass, he was quiet. "Cheering, please," I requested as I stood up on the pedals and set my mind and body to the task.

"Go, Mom! You can do it, Mom. Remember your power. Remember all the good things you eat that give you energy," Chan called out without hesitation. "Remember all the good things you've done. You can do it." His words helped me to press down hard again and again, with each stroke of the pedals. I felt my muscles strain and overwork, but I didn't give up. "Feel the energy. Draw the energy up from the earth. Up your legs and down your legs. Up and down. Up and down. More energy. You can do it, Mom!"

Sweat soaked my hair under the helmet. My hands gripped the handlebars tight. The strain felt like it would be too much, but I kept pushing, one downward thrust at a time.

I couldn't believe it. We'd made it. All the way up that long steep road over loose, dry dirt and dead grass.

"Honey, we did it! I never could have done that without your cheering. Did you know you are an amazing cheerer. If you cheer like that for yourself, you'll be over your cancer in no time!"

~~~

DAP

~~~

DAYS LATER, A VOICE CAME ECHOING over the valley from the far ridge. At first we thought it wasn't for us, then Dtaw could make out Cam's words across the distance: "Come see Dap! The rope got tangled around his neck!" My stomach lurched as Dtaw walked up to the house to get his machete and muttered over Cam's inability to take care of horses. I imagined the huge animal dangling over some edge by the rough rope caught around its neck. The horrible thought haunted me for hours. It felt like too much; I had enough fear of immediate death around me. I couldn't take any more.

The first thing Chan said was, "Don't blame me for buying the horses; I'd help care for them if I could."

Hours later Dtaw came back. As usual, he didn't offer information till pressed.

"No, he wasn't dead, but he'd been stuck in the rope all night, and in the morning Cam found him lying down. He lay down all morning, but by the time I got there, he was standing."

Later, when I saw Cam, he was more eager to share details, perhaps to relieve some of his guilt. "I found him belly up, his legs up in the air. I splashed water on him, and rubbed lemongrass under his nose to revive him. He woke, but didn't stand until the afternoon. This evening he was able to walk back here with the other horses."

Earlier that afternoon, when we had gone out walking, I told Cody what had happened. "The moral of the story is that one shouldn't own horses if one doesn't have time to care for them," I said, trying to relieve my own guilt. I hadn't realized Cam was keeping them on the steep hillside he tilled daily. If I had seen the situation, I would have known the danger, but I wonder if I would have held out against Cam's and Dtaw's *never mind* attitudes. In Thai, there is a phrase that most visitors learn before any other: *mai pen rai*. It means *no problem, never mind, there's nothing to worry about, relax*. It's the phrase used for *you're welcome* and every other situation when the foreigner feels worry and anxiety, and the local smiles and reminds him or her that everything will be okay. *Don't worry so much*. So many times I heard that response to my worries that I learned to question *any* worries and concerns I had. Were they legitimate or was it my American habit of overthinking, of seeing the worst-case scenario, of trying to control the future? I was worried all along about owning horses when we knew nothing about it, about entrusting them to someone who had only raised water buffaloes and pigs and chickens and ducks. But I gave up fighting with Dtaw about this before I even started because I knew what he would say: *mai pen rai*.

This time, though, Dtaw was also angry that he had allowed Cam to keep them there overnight against Dtaw's request. Cam had protested that it was too much work to bring them back and forth, so Dtaw had relented. Cody, after going to see the horses, told me that Dap's upper lip was hanging down loose over his teeth, and he didn't seem well. I imagined he suffered some brain damage from lack of oxygen during his ordeal, but I was no vet, and I had enough to worry about without adding Dap's life expectancy to my list.

SOUP

THE NEXT MORNING I THOUGHT CHAN might be drawing his last breaths. After he woke up, he waited for me to finish cooking the rice so I could go up and get him for breakfast. I did so, carefully pulling the sleeves over his swollen and tender hands and the turtleneck over his sore ears and nose. I went outside to shoo the horses away from the bathwater jar they liked to drink from, and by the time I went back in the hut to carry him down to the kitchen, he had fallen asleep.

I quietly left him and ducked my head as I passed through the small door of the dark kitchen to make rice soup. Taking down the chipped enamel plate that held the bones and head of the small grilled fish Cody had eaten for dinner, I slid them into the dented aluminum pot half filled with rainwater. Tahn and Cody had already headed off to Tong's house shortly before dawn to catch their favorite Sunday-morning cartoons. I only let them go because I wanted Chan to be able to sleep longer after his long night of discomfort when he didn't give in to morphine till well past midnight. He was sure it wasn't pain that was keeping him awake but something else. I didn't like giving him morphine for anxiety, but I didn't know what else to do. Early in the morning he woke for a few minutes and said, "I'm glad I took the morphine. It really helped me sleep."

While I was savoring the quiet pleasure of cooking and eating my soup without distraction from the other boys, Chan's voice, faint with fatigue, called for me, letting me know he was ready to get up. By the time I got up the four steps to our room, he had fallen asleep again. I returned to my soup, sprinkling fried garlic the color of gold over the steaming surface. He called for me again. This time when I looked through the small doorway, he was barely awake. His eyes flickered at me, seemed to recognize me, and fell shut again. His breaths were long and labored. I pulled down the collar of his red turtleneck to look for a pulse below the swollen glands. I consoled myself that my other boys' breathing sounded that way when they had nasal congestion, as Chan did. I sat with him, holding his slender hand, reassuring him I was nearby, wondering if Dtaw should phone down to the village to have Cam race up on the motorcycle with Cody and Tahn so they could be here before Chan died. After I sat with him and watched him a little longer, his breath steadied, he slept peacefully, and I decided I could go back downstairs.

The next time he woke up, he said he wanted to go to the kitchen. I offered the hammock which was sunnier. Tears streamed down as he said, "No! I said the kitchen. I hate it when you keep offering me things!"

"Okay, okay."

So I set up the bedding on the worn wooden floor-boards of the small windowless room that was our kitchen. He surprised me by choosing to sit up and then proceeded to drink a cup of apple vegetable juice with protein powder, some crackers made of crispy sticky rice, one tangerine, and half a jicama. *Do dying people have such an appetite?* I wondered. He cried and slept and cried and slept all morning. While he slept, I worried about his dying, so rather than doing outdoor chores, I sat near him and made applesauce by the warm fire.

Dtaw's brother had sent us a whole box of apples, big and red, from China. I shuddered to think what kind of chemicals they had been treated with. I soaked three of them, bobbing together stem up, a floating chubby triangle in the large stainless steel bowl. Apples in the tropics are rarely crunchy, and these were no exception. Being just shy of mealy, however, made the motion of slicing sections off with my small sharp knife satisfying. Each time I was left with an irregular polygon outline around the core, which was up to me to nibble into the normal shape of apple remains. I filled the pot, shiny silver on the inside, smoke-blackened on the outside, with rainwater, halfway to the level of the apples, settled it carefully over the orange glowing coals, and waited.

Chan sat, his neck jutting out, pushing his head strangely forward, as if it was too heavy to hold up. It looked to me as if he had gone from child to old man in the space of only one night. He seemed only half awake and answered questions half-heartedly.

In the evening when I had some time with him, I tried to get through to him. He sat in my lap, stubbornly avoiding my gaze, unwilling to let me in enough to cry as I knew he would once he opened to my presence. I told him how I loved him, how amazing he was, how I was sure he'd get well, how everything was going to be okay.

No dice, just eyes rolling up into his head or away from my gaze. I stood up at the foot of the hammock, looking at him with what was (apparently) a loving gaze. That brought some reaction and I moved in close again.

"Are you worried about something?"

Barely perceptible nod of head as eyes rolled upward.

"Are you worried about being sick?"

Same answer.

"Are you worried you're never going to get well?"

Same answer.

I paused, considering, before diving in with the next question. "Are you worried you'll die?"

He too paused and then gave a very small, but definite shake of his head, not in denial, but slowly and thoughtfully.

I moved along: "You'll get well, honey, everything will be okay."

When I finally stopped and was quiet for a few minutes, he said very quietly, "And I worry that you're going to . . . going to die." And at last the tears flowed. "I don't want to be a grown-up!"

"Because then I'll die?"

He nodded. "I would just miss you so much. I just really love you."

Those wide brown eyes turned on me, the love and fear of losing what he loved flowing out of them with the tears. I reassured him that I wasn't going anywhere, that I didn't have any enemies and there were no murderers in the village.

"Except tigers," he said. "But you might get a disease."

"Oh, but honey, I've learned so much from you about how to fight disease and never give up that I'm not even worried about getting sick or getting cancer. I'll just do what I learned from you."

He was still scared. I told him that no matter what happens, when two people love each other, even death can't separate them; that when I die, I'll still be with him, a part of him. As I talked so bravely and philosophically about death and grief, the tears were streaming down my own face.

What was it that made him so fearful then? Did he pick up my constant fear about our separation? Whenever I brought up the subject of his death, it seemed like it wasn't an issue he was considering. He really just seemed to think the worst thing that could happen would be that he'd have cancer for the rest of his very long life. When I asked him one other time if he ever thought about dying, he replied immediately, "Yeah. It would be cool to be a cheetah or some animal in my next life if I didn't get hunted."

NEAR

*I*N THE MORNING WHILE CHAN NAPPED, I rushed, as I always did, to creep quietly away from him to pull my laptop from its bag, settle myself into a nest of cotton quilts, and begin the exhalation of typing. Writing. Without it, I would not have survived, I think. I had to purge the fears, the pain, the moments that otherwise were too much for me, pouring all of it out through my fingertips into the keyboard, releasing regularly what was otherwise too much to bear.

The sun had climbed high enough in the sky to warm my legs folded beneath me as I sat on the porch typing. Dap munched contentedly on the long grass next to the garbage pit. I had to glance up now and then to make sure he didn't start on the young vegetables Dtaw and Tong had planted near the water jars. He was not the same horse he had been before the fall. He wandered separate from his friends, close to the house to drink water from the bath jar.

Chan woke and called to me. I went in to find him still lying down in the darkened bedroom, his thinning hair wet with sweat and his lips nearly white dry, teeth clotted with coagulated blood. I thought this blood was from his cracked lips the way it was so dry and scabby, but the Bangkok nutritionist I'd called days before for advice reminded me that people with leukemia bleed from the gums.

I was beginning, finally, to understand why talking about death with Chan, or even in relation to Chan, was such a completely abhorrent and alien concept in the culture where we were. I realized that if we lived where there was no doctor and no one to tell me what illness my child was living through, I would simply do my very best to take care of him, giving him all the most effective remedies I knew about, giving him love and encouragement and doing all I could to heal him. I wouldn't think, *Oh, he might die, so why bother.* Death wouldn't even be something I would give much thought to until it happened. I would just fight and fight and fight until I could fight no more.

I think in the West, we have grown up knowing only when doctors' predictions about cancer come true. It is part of our cultural language to equate cancer with death. We read books about it. We join support groups. We do things we've put off for too long. We mend broken relationships. There's a whole world of how to handle terminal illness because for so long we have had doctors who have been predicting the outcome of our illnesses and most often been right. In Thailand, however, this word *cancer* is new. Doctors have not had long to prove themselves right, and often are still highly mistrusted. The cultural way of handling disease has not yet caught up to the realities of Western medicine.

Once I understood this reluctance to speak of death

with Chan as something that came not from fear, but instead from a rational view of how to care for a patient, I was much more amenable to the traditional village approach. *Yes*, I told myself, *I will continue to fight for Chan. I will continue to feed him healing foods and herbs and vitamins. I will continue to talk to him about his future.* There was no reason to give up. I would still fight. *He might get well or he might die*, I thought. How could it ever be sensible to say, *Okay, honey, I have now surmised from the way you look or the fact that you nap too much or that your lips are too dry that you will soon die, and there is no point in hoping for anything else?* Given the cultural context, that would be ludicrous. I finally began to see why I got such blank looks from Tong when I told her I thought Chan was about to die. How ridiculous that I should presume to know such a thing. No one can predict the future. We just do the best we can with what we have right now.

As I typed, away from the duties of caring for Chan, the heaviness in my limbs, the ache in my shoulders and back from bending, tending, lifting, spoke to me of my own fatigue. I noticed the relief I felt in Chan's new quiet passivity as he napped more. Guilt quickly followed. I felt grateful when I thought that his death might be slow and gentle rather than violent and painful, and guilty that I was enjoying having more time to write, more time to tidy up, more time to myself. I was able to do more than only listen to Chan scream and cry. It upset me that I seemed to be in such a hurry for him to die neatly and quietly.

I had noticed the day before that Chan's abdomen was covered with tiny purple petechiae. I was tempted to hide them from Dtaw, worrying that he'd want to put Chan through the ordeal of going to Bangkok to a hated

CATHARINE H. MURRAY ~ 225

hospital to get platelets. I was so wedded to this idea of a nice simple quiet death, no hospitals, no traffic, no cities. It seemed wrong, like I didn't even want to help Chan if it was going to make things more complicated. I knew I tended to be hard on myself, so I decided to try to look at this in a way other than the obsessive control-oriented mother wanting her child to hurry up and die so she could get her life back in order.

At that point the fear felt worse than the current reality, maybe because the torture is in the fact that it might not happen, that you might get to watch your child grow up and have a girlfriend and be really good at sports and use his brilliant brain and be a dad and love to build things. The torture is keeping hope for all of that alive, but knowing you probably won't get it. Death seemed easier, final, over. There would be no room for hope. I could just sink into utter grief and despair. No more needing to figure anything out. I could just give up and be a total victim of the misery of life. Holding the possibility and hope for a long and loving life with the child I was so close to and the possibility and fear of his death in one heart at the same time was just too hard, and I'd been doing it for so long.

It was hard because . . . I don't know. Isn't that the whole basis of suffering? Desire and aversion? Chan was tortured by how much he loved me and feared losing me. Is this the crux of our existence? Fear of losing what we love? I tried so hard to learn something from this puzzle, something to lift me above the tangle of it all, but I kept coming up feeling blank and stupid, my brain refusing to move, the cogs stuck. *Maybe there is no philosophical escape*, I thought. *Maybe it is just plain sad and hard and the only way over is through. It might be okay to be very sad here,* I told myself. My thoughts, transforming into printed words before my eyes, instructed me so that I could allow myself the blessed relief of tears.

I listened to Chan snoring quietly, nose congested. For days he'd been blowing chunks of bloody snot out of his nose into endless rolls of toilet paper, using a long sheet for only a few dabs of blood. I saw it as his body slowly coming apart from the inside. Dtaw and Chan persisted in calling these bits of him toxins, Chan questioningly, Dtaw with certainty. When Chan's poop revealed what looked to me like a piece of his intestine, white and pink and slimy, Dtaw pronounced it a toxin.

I wondered if it was weird that the sicker Chan got, the more I felt compelled to write it all down. I had some reasons. I wanted to hold on to every second while Chan was still alive. I knew from experience that I would forget so much. Already, I had almost entirely forgotten his infancy and toddlerhood, so if he disappeared forever, I was afraid all my memories would fade quickly as well. I wanted to remember what an amazing human being he was and what a close relationship we had, how much we loved each other.

Another reason was that I was sure that when he did die, I would be unable to write. I was afraid the grief would be so crushing that I would not be able to sit down and sort it out the way I did then, fingers tapping the keys almost as fast as my thoughts spoke themselves into nothingness inside me. And finally, writing gave me some distance from all of it. Whether it pushed the experience toward the world of fiction, removing me from its center, or whether it just let me stand back a bit, allowing me to breathe outside of it, or whether it let me package it all up neatly and tightly into words and paper so that I could contain and control this uncontainable, uncontrollable piece of life, I don't know. But whatever the reason, it helped to keep me sane, so I wrote whenever I could find the time. I thought maybe someday, someone else could benefit from my thoughts—but then, I couldn't see how. I thought, *It's enough for me to benefit.*

Chan slept on his side facing me as always, his thin legs bent and resting on a large soft pillow. His swollen hands sought out my arm or chest or face, any piece of me to touch as he slept.

He woke often, needing water for his parched mouth, needing to pee, but most often to be sure I was turned toward him. Once around midnight, after we had turned off the flashlight and settled down again to sleep, he reached out to stroke my head and looked at me with his big eyes and whispered, his voice soft and breaking, "I just love you so much, Mom. I would just miss you so much if you died. I'm so glad you're my mom. We'll be together forever. We'll die together, right?"

"Of course we will," I said. I figured when he was taking his last breaths I'd be able to ask his permission to live on to take care of the other boys. "We'll always be together, honey. When we're older than *Mei Tu* (great-grandmother), we'll die together, okay?"

"Okay. I just love you *so* much. I'm so glad you let me cry. I'm glad you're not a Thai mom, because then you wouldn't let me cry."

I pointed out that some Thai moms let their kids cry and many American moms don't.

Then he said, "I love you more than the earth."

"I love you too, honey. I'm so lucky to have you."

"I'm lucky to have you," Chan continued in this terribly grave and almost awed tone, like he just couldn't fathom how much he loved me and how terrified he was of losing me. At last he finished with, "I love nature too. I love all the animals."

TOO MUCH

A COOL BREEZE RUFFLED CHAN'S silky brown hair. I marveled at how soft and sweet-smelling it was, though it had been weeks that the pain had kept us from washing it. I brought a bowl of cold spring water with two fresh washcloths and his toothbrush up to the bedroom where he had been confined by his pain for several days, then carefully wiped the tender skin stretched over his thin bones. The pelvic bones surprised me most, how large and shallow their oblong disks appeared under his skin.

He asked me to hurry as he was getting cold, so I quickly put the sleeping bag back over him, then slowly brushed his teeth, noting that his gums weren't bleeding much, only enough to make the foam he spit into the small metal bowl a little pink.

Wearing a fresh T-shirt, one with a wide collar to fit over his sore ears and nose, he asked for oatmeal. I cooked it, worrying that, as often happened, by the time I brought it back to him, he would be fast asleep, but he was wide awake and waiting. To my amazement, he finished nearly the whole big portion I served him, with plenty of brown sugar that I added since Dtaw was not here to forbid it and because I knew it would help more of the oatmeal go down. Full, he said he would nap and then eat some fish and rice and boiled eggs afterward. For the last week or so, he hadn't woken up to eat breakfast until around noon.

Chan lay emaciated in our bed with his face like an old man's. I was finishing wiping a washcloth over his naked body. Dtaw had gone to pick up Cody from school at lunchtime so Chan wouldn't have to wait for him so long. When Cody came into the room, I think the shock of seeing how thin Chan's naked body was made him burst out crying. He said it was because he had so much homework, but I thought at the time that because Cody hadn't really seen Chan without clothes much lately, the sight just broke his heart.

Chan said, "You can go listen to Cody," after Cody stormed out of the room. So I did. I fought and struggled with him as he screamed and cried about his "homework." Finally he hit me on the head with his schoolbook, which was the point where I always lost my temper, so I left. That was the end of his cry.

I came back to Chan, and soon Cody followed me, bringing his math book to work out the problems next to me as I tried to feed Chan some grilled fish. Cody soon gave up on getting any help from me, and left with his unfinished homework. I pulled bits of tender meat away from the fine bones of the mackerel, whole and crispy from the fire, to press between Chan's cracked lips, but the tears wouldn't stop flowing down my face as I thought about Cody's sadness.

Chan sat up in bed, his shoulders hunched forward, his shrunken head jutting out from the exhaustion of trying to hold it up. "It's okay, Mom, you can go cry with Daddy." He said this gently and lovingly a couple of times as I struggled to control my tears.

"Does that mean you don't want to listen to me cry?" I joked, smiling between the tears.

"You can cry with me," he said. "It's good to cry. Go ahead." The sweetness and gentleness with which he said these words in such an adult way brought the sobbing on even harder, and he lifted his bony arm to put around my shoulder. I moved in closer and laid my head against his chest, careful not to bump any of his painful parts. "It's good to cry, Mom. Just keep crying. Cry as much as you want to. You can always cry with me. It's good to cry with your children. Just keep crying."

I couldn't stop myself. I sobbed so hard into his lap and said, "I just love you so much. There's no one like you in the whole world." The words I had to keep biting back, though, were, *Please, please don't die, Chan. I really don't want you to die.*

Despite his repeated encouragement to keep crying, I stopped after a few minutes, feeling much better than before and amazed at Chan's ability and willingness to do that for me.

A few days later, I mentioned what a great job he had done listening to me and how much it helped.

"When I feel stronger, I can listen to you again, Mom. Just today I feel too weak."

"I know, baby."

~~

SWEET THINGS

~~

WE CELEBRATED TAHN'S THIRD BIRTHDAY on December 18, 2004. I was proud of the pineapple tart I managed to make on the covered pan over the fire. With flaxseed, oat, and sunflower seed crust, it was crunchy and sweet with the fresh chunks of pineapple on top. Dtaw's mom and brother came just in time to sign the card I'd made and deliver the Christmas and Tahn's birthday presents my brother Dave, his wife Vivian, and my mother had sent through the mail. I couldn't believe how happy and animated Chan became over all his Christmas presents. He smiled, and said out loud to the sky, "Thanks, Dave and Viv, I love you!" and, "Thanks, Grammy, I miss you!" And he shouted over each of his presents as he opened them. "YES! Cheerios! YES! The Kim Possible video game!" And best of all, when he opened a gorgeously illustrated children's book about one of the greatest miracle makers in history, he cheered, "YES! Gandhi!" I couldn't believe it. He was usually so listless and sad. The entire day amazed me. He asked to go down to the village in the trailer to watch his favorite show about a ten-year-old village boy with superhero powers. A total surprise to me—only forty-eight hours ago I'd thought he was at the end of his life.

After the excitement of the presents, things quieted down as we all shared a dinner of noodle soup on the porch floor. It was dark and late when Chan finally begged to go to bed. We sang happy birthday to Tahn and he loved it. He said he wanted to hear it again. When I gave him his card, he looked at it and asked for more. He took awhile to blow out his candles, but was finally successful. We quickly ate the tart and got everybody into bed. Mei Ya and Dtaw's brother Giat were gone by the time we started reading *Harry Potter and the Sorcerer's Stone*.

The next day Chan was very worried about his swollen toes. I'd rubbed them and elevated them and put hot herbal compresses on them. I called the palliative care nurse from Seattle Children's Hospital. Standing among the broken rice stalks in the field above the cabin where there was decent cell reception, I listened as she explained that the swelling could be leukemia in the feet or it could be leukemia in the kidneys or it could be the weakened heart just not able to pump the blood well enough to the extremities and organs. I hoped it was only lack of use and maybe we'd be able to get them working again. Chan wanted so badly to stand. Later he struggled up, leaning on me, hoping to be able to get upright. His legs were far too weak, of course.

For days Chan had been begging for sun-dried bananas. I was too busy worrying about which day would be his last to take time to fulfill this small request. But Tong listened. Back at home, she told me later, she carried her machete into the jungle and came out with a thick green stem heavy with bunches of bananas, like hands curled over each other. In her hard-dirt yard, she set to work among the pecking hens. Peeling each banana, she dropped the fruit onto a circular tray of woven bamboo strips darkened with age, and covered them with stiff blue netting to keep the birds and flies away. These she set atop the low corrugated tin roof of the kitchen to catch the afternoon sun.

After two days, they were ready. Sliding the trays off the roof and briskly shooing the chickens that had followed at her heels, Tong carried them into the kitchen where she stoked the fire in the bucket stove and set the water to boil in the wide-bellied pot. On the lip that flared around the rim, she set the conical basket used so many times a day for steaming rice, vegetables, tubers, jungle crabs, and now bananas. She laid down each one, shrunken and golden from the sun, leaving space for the steam to swirl evenly through. She adjusted the burning sticks in the fire to create a low blaze.

Later, lifting the dented lid from the basket and squinting through the smoke and steam, Tong pushed her fingertips against the sweating fruit to check their softness. Calling to Cam to ready the motorcycle, she wrapped the warm fruit in sections of banana leaf. Cam came and stooped in the low doorframe, forearm resting above his head, the darkening afternoon sky behind him.

When the bananas were ready, Tong and Cam left their home for ours. Up over the rutted dirt they rode, past the fields that rolled away, yellow and brown, down to the valley below.

~~~

CHANGE

~~~

*C*HAN SAT ON HIS MAKESHIFT DAYTIME BED, colorful flat square cushions lined up to hold his thin body above the rough planks of the porch. With a low railing around three sides, our porch was big enough for all of us to sit together. Chan loved to watch the jungle below—the distant waves of mountains far across the valley and the white puffs of cloud that chased across the sky. He had sat like this for weeks.

Too weak to walk, he had to be carried everywhere: down the hill to see the horses in their pasture, up the path above our cabin to watch the birds that floated below, into the clearing to lie back and gaze up at the spindly treetops, soaking in the quiet of the sunny jungle here in the middle of the universe. But in the last few days, he had been growing more and more tired, and even thinner. And the night fevers had gotten so high that I couldn't find the end of the silver bar of mercury in the glass of the thermometer. It didn't matter. There was nothing we could do.

We went on with life. I took the bedding out to air like I did every day, removing the sheets, soaked each night in sweat from the fevers that raged through my boy's flesh. I gathered up the thick comforters filled with fresh cotton, plucked and matted by our neighbors in town, and stuffed them out the small wooden window frame to air out on the warm tin roof of the kitchen. In the wind and mountain sunshine of the dry season, they were always fresh and light again by lunchtime.

Two days after Tahn's birthday, I was in the bedroom, a few steps away from Chan who was seated on the porch. I had brought the sheets and blankets back in and laid them in a pile in the small margin of floor next to the bed. As I raised a fresh sheet swirling above my head to spread onto the bed, I turned to look out the narrow door to where Chan sat. He looked somehow amiss. His skull jutted out in front of his torso. His body listed to the left. I thought of Dap's slack-jawed face. I left my work and went to my son. His eyes and tongue seemed to be roaming from side to side. Something about it spelled out brain damage to me, and I could only imagine that the cancer had spread into his brain.

He was trying to play with his toy trucks. He asked me to bring all of them. I said I already had. He shook his head slowly, as if with effort to think and speak, and said, "No. Another."

I glanced around, panic rising as I tried again to succeed at giving him what he needed. I went down the steps and found the missing vehicle, a small space shuttle, beside where Tahn was playing in the dirt. I hurried up to place it on the low table over Chan's lap. Mystified by this change in him, I watched him try to play, his hands suddenly clumsy, as if too big to control. I waited, counting to ten, coaching myself to be patient. I checked the urge to reach out and help him load the space shuttle onto the tractor trailer, wanting him to still feel independent, powerful. Three-year-old Tahn bounced up the steps and tried to grab the backhoe from Chan. I told him to stop, and Chan said in his thickening speech, "We share, Tahn, remember, we share." With something crippling his brain before my eyes, how, I asked myself, could he remember this golden rule?

Tahn gave in and the two boys played quietly together. I called to Dtaw to take a video of them, but he didn't. I didn't bother hounding him about it. I wish I had. I asked Chan to lie down to rest, but as weak as he looked, he refused.

"Mama, are we going to the hospital tomorrow?" he asked.

"Yes, honey. I think it would be a good idea to get some red blood cells into you."

He started to cry then. "I hate it when they treat me like a baby!"

I assured him we wouldn't let them.

"Why do the nurses here *do* that?" he asked me. "I hate it when they do that."

I had no answer.

Chan cried more, talking about how hard he'd been trying to get well. He said, "I used to love it when Tahn came to see me at the hospital in Seattle because he'd always hug me when he got there." This sent him into fresh tears. "I used to love Tahn so much when he was little, but then he turned into a bully."

I told him that deep down Tahn wasn't a bully, he just watched too many fighting cartoons and played too many Ninja Turtles video games.

As Chan's crying slowed, Cody, who had wandered up

to the porch when he heard the crying, lay down next to Chan and said, "I don't care if Tahn's mean, I just wish Chan didn't get leukemia."

"Me too," I agreed.

Chan spoke up: "The one good thing about leukemia is that I learned about my power." Then, smiling as if he had a special secret, he added, "You know what I love more than you, Mom?"

"No. What?"

"My power."

After a little while, Chan began to cry about how he missed his grandmother. "I want my Grammy! I want to see your mama! I miss Grammy!" He went on with this heartbroken talk until I was crying too. We assured him she was coming to visit soon.

"When?" he demanded.

"In three weeks," I answered.

"How many days is that?"

"Twenty-one."

"No, Mama," Cody called from the bedroom where he had gone to consult the calendar, "it's only nineteen days from now."

"How many is nineteen?" Chan asked.

"That's all your fingers and toes except for one," I told him.

"Just tell her to come soon! I want to see Grammy. I love Grammy! I miss Grammy."

I kept hugging him and crying as he cried. When the tide subsided, we sat quietly for a few minutes.

Then with a new round of grief, he said, "I miss my Uncle Dave and my Aunt Vivian and little David." This time the tears fell even harder. "I just want my aunt and uncle and baby! When are they coming? Tell them to hurry and come see me!"

Eventually he progressed to, "I love Aunt Vivian the most! She always helped me and we did origami together. I love her more than anybody." After this outpouring of grief, he calmed down and asked me to bring him the postcards he had picked out on our last trip to the city. I brought them and he picked out one for Dave and Vivian and little David. He then dictated while I filled the card with his words, mostly telling them how much he would like to see them. He asked for one to write to Grammy, but by the time he had chosen one, he was too tired to dictate, and asked me to help him lie down. Seeing me get the morphine from the shelf, he questioned if it was okay to take it. "I don't want to die," he said matter-of-factly.

I was taken aback and said, "What, honey? What do you mean?"

"I mean about the morphine and the breathing."

I reassured him that a little bit would be okay. He dutifully swallowed the small brown pills I held out to him and soon fell asleep.

We heard the buzz of the motorcycle before we saw it. Cody and Tahn called out as they always did, "Mei Tong ma laow!" (Mama Tong is coming!) The boys ran to meet Paw Cam and Mei Tong as their motorcycle chugged up over the rise toward our house. Chan stirred and wakened. I looked up toward Cam and Tong, relieved. Finally, some help. They would look at Chan and tell me what to do. But they only came to him and smiled, Tong announcing, "Gluay tak!" (Sun-dried bananas!)

Chan smiled, happy as always to see his second set of

parents. Head jutting out too far in front and tilted oddly, he said, *"Khap jai lai lai"* (Thank you so much) to Mei Tong in her mountain dialect.

As soon as she put the plate of sticky fruit in front of him, he began to shove the bananas into his mouth one by one. I was amazed by such an appetite. How could my boy who seemed to be so close to death eat like that? But I was not reassured.

The way his fingers fumbled clumsily into his slackening mouth haunted me afterward. His head and hands swung toward each other in their effort to eat with the uncertainty of the limbs of a marionette. I'd never seen him eat with such greed. What made him press one small banana after another into his mouth, as if he'd never get his favorite treat again?

Even as I worried, I watched and smiled at this small pleasure, this moment of freedom from pain, this moment of a little boy's simple enjoyment of food. But I knew I could not stay in that moment for long.

SCARED

WHEN DTAW CAME IN FROM HIS WORK planting trees later in the afternoon, I pulled him aside. "I think Chan is dying and I'm scared and I don't know what to do," I said. He looked at me with his usual loving skepticism. I told him I had promised Chan we'd go to the hospital the next day for red blood cells. "I just want things to be simple," I said. "I'm afraid we'll get there and the nurses and doctors will freak out and put him in ICU and give him oxygen and not let us leave."

"We'll just get the blood and come home. Not stay overnight."

"Are you sure we can make that happen?"

"Yes."

"Do you really think the red blood cells will help?" I asked, not because I was wondering. I was sure they wouldn't. But if Dtaw truly believed that they would, I didn't see how I could deny him the chance to try to save Chan's life or at least make him more comfortable. If he felt we could help our boy with the transfusion, then we had to try. I explained that because of the way Chan seemed to have slowed and drooped, I thought the cancer had reached the brain. I said nothing we could do would help now, and what if he needed platelets, then would we take him to Bangkok? But that was only borrowing trouble. We agreed that we would go to the provincial capital for blood the next day.

That night I readied Chan's usual space in the middle of the bed, a small clean baby blanket over a baby pad in case he wet the sheets, though that hadn't happened yet. We lay down together facing each other, arranging our legs just right so that I wouldn't hurt his tender limbs while we slept. I bent my knees toward him, then he carefully placed his bottom leg, hardly more than a few long bones, between my soft thighs, then his other leg on top of the stack.

After we said good night and how much we loved each other and made sure the other was comfortable and all was quiet, I sensed him making the painful and difficult effort of moving his arm so that his small hand could reach over and rest gently against the skin of my chest, so he could feel my warm skin on his own. That night he had the best night's sleep he'd had in a long time.

In the morning when he woke up, Chan's speech was more slurred than ever, but we were still able to understand him. He insisted on having his shorts put on because he didn't want the nurses to tease him, pointing to his penis, laughing, *Joo, joo*. Despite the pain in his toes, we managed to get him dressed and into the car. He had made it clear the day before that he wanted Cody to go with him to the hospital. We had some indecision over whether to take Tahn. There was always the worry that when we took Chan to the hospital he might die there, and then I wanted his brothers to be with him. Last time all five of us had gone for a transfusion. Tong came too, despite her aversion to car rides, to give Chan her blood because there was no match for him left in the province that day. After that trip, with toddler needs, crankiness, and car sickness on top of all the other stress, I concluded this time that a small crowd was more than I could handle. We decided to leave Tahn at home with Cam and Tong.

After I slowly settled myself and Chan into the front seat of the Land Rover, he said to me in a voice becoming less and less intelligible, "Make sure we buy gum on the way."

He was looking forward to going, to the ritual of driving down through the mountains, going out for meals, and having a whole day of undivided attention from me. As the car jolted and bumped its way down the rough road from our house toward the village, I worried that Chan would hurt from all the bouncing. He looked up at me and asked, deep concern showing in his eyes, "Are you comfortable, Mama?" He had been spending so much time on my lap in the last weeks that he had gotten into the habit of always checking to see if *I* was comfortable.

By seven a.m. we were in front of Tong's house. The van Dtaw had arranged to meet us was waiting with doors open. The usual neighbors were there, adults trying tactfully not to stare and children openly doing so as I lifted Chan's emaciated body wrapped in the sleeping bag carefully down from the Land Rover. Chan was in pain, but patient. Before I lifted him into the van, I called Tahn over and made sure that he had a chance to kiss Chan goodbye and tell him he loved him. Tahn did as I asked, but it took awhile for him to understand that I wanted him to say those three words.

Once in the van, we settled into the seat behind the driver, Dtaw on my left, Chan on my lap with his head resting on Dtaw's shoulder, and Cody behind us. Chan soon fell asleep, and I tried to make sure he was well covered in the cold morning air without putting any pressure on his swollen foot. Cody was helpful and cheerful all the way to the city despite throwing up in a plastic bag as we neared the hospital. Chan mostly slept.

When we arrived at the hospital, there was more indecision about whether to go in the emergency entrance so he could have a stretcher and therefore be moved as little as possible, or whether to go in a wheelchair in the front entrance so I could protect him from bumps. In the end, I decided he'd be safer in my lap in the wheelchair. We were met by the doctor who was familiar with Chan's case, and given a private room.

The same nurse who had had the difficult job of trying to find a vein that night Chan got poked ten times was on duty and she inserted the needle to take his blood count. Chan didn't seem to register the pain of the poke, making me realize how far he was beginning to slip from his normal state. We asked the doctor about Chan's toe and he offered protein, but thought we'd need to do a venesection to administer it. We declined.

We decided to put him on the gurney instead of my lap so we could elevate his painful toe. When we moved him, he moaned but then returned to sleep. We propped his foot up on two fat pillows and covered him with the sleeping bag. Chan continued to sleep while we waited for the results of the CBC. He woke several times and asked for water or to pee. Speaking had become a struggle, and the words came out in long high-pitched moans through straight lips so that we had to strain to understand. But he still seemed aware of what was going on.

By now we had to yell for Chan to hear us. When we did, he would open his eyes wide and seemed to understand. His face had become oddly thinner, drawn, and an unfamiliar crease gashed his face to the right of his mouth.

After a while, an attendant wheeled the gurney up to the fifth floor and led us to room 503. He was kind enough to leave Chan on the gurney rather than risk more pain by moving him onto the bed. Chan spent the day mostly sleeping quietly. I stayed by his head, stroking his hair, there when he woke up to reassure him. I sat beside him, straining to make contact with him when he opened his eyes, to let him know I was right there. An oddly quiet state descended on me while he slept. I began to see in my mind the light of the deep cosmos filled with countless stars, a place that felt inconceivably distant, yet so vast it would be all-encompassing. I spoke to Chan with all the calm conviction I'd ever had as I sat with him. "You are going to be okay, sweetie. The universe is a good place. Wherever you are going, you will be okay."

Mei Ya and three of Dtaw's brothers all came to see Chan, spending a few hours with us. He was aware that they were there and opened his eyes wide, looking wildly about him, to take in each of them, one by one, while they shouted their words of reassurance to him that he would get well. It must have been their way of saying goodbye.

While Dtaw sat with Chan, I took a long hot shower. Cody watched a *Harry Potter* movie out on the balcony on the laptop. I didn't press him to come in. I imagined all this was too hard for him to witness. Now I wish I hadn't left him alone while Chan was leaving us.

In the afternoon, Dtaw took Cody out for lunch. I stayed close to Chan as he slept. He lay in the bed, only barely conscious. When Dtaw and Cody returned, I wanted to wash Chan's hair. Dtaw brought washcloths and a basin of warm water from the bathroom to bathe him and lifted his head as I washed our child's hair. Chan only woke up to moan a few times as I poured the silky water over his head, glad to have it clean.

By the time all the blood had dripped into his body and he had on clean clothes and Dtaw's family had gone back home, it had gotten dark and cool outside. The doctor agreed that he could be taken home. Cody helped me gather our things as we waited for the attendant to roll Chan's gurney back downstairs and out the glass doors to where the minivan was waiting, engine running. In the cool night air of the hospital driveway, I leaned down and lifted Chan into my arms, stepping into the van and sliding onto the backseat, mindful as always of his swollen and painful feet. As far away as he seemed to be now from the pain that had tormented him for so long, I still did not want to risk hurting him.

I settled us into place and Chan's eyes opened. His jaws, now tightened by the strange change in his muscle-to-brain connection, worked and his mouth moved. His eyes rolled as he tried to speak. Only unintelligible sounds issued from his lips as he grew more and more urgent, trying to tell me something.

"What is it, honey? What do you want?" I kept asking, pained that I couldn't answer to his needs. "Are you uncomfortable? Are you hungry? Do you need some water?" With each question, I searched his face. He seemed to say no. He waved his stiff arms with their strangely bent fingers, trying hard to communicate. Exasperated, desperate, I asked Cody beside me and Dtaw in the front, "What does he want? Help me understand." Each of them sat silent, unable to answer.

And then I felt the familiar warmth of a baby on my lap as wetness soaked through my jeans. He had been trying to tell me he had to pee. He didn't want to wet my clothes. I was relieved that was all it was, though I ached at how he worried about inconveniencing me in that moment. We found a towel, slipped off his wet shorts, and dried him off before starting for the mountain.

He drifted back to sleep or the distant place he'd been as we drove through the dark. I held him close. Cody leaning against me as he and Dtaw slept. The driver and I sat awake and silent. Three hours later, we reached Tong's house where the Land Rover was parked. Every window in the village was dark. Climbing out into the cool night, holding Chan, I saw him wake and look around. He seemed content, knowing where he was. With Dtaw at the wheel, the Land Rover rumbled up the rutted road home. Chan lay in my arms, awake and calm.

He'd always loved that old Land Rover. He would speak up in its defense whenever I complained about the lack of shock absorbers or the way its ancient engine guzzled gas. That night he knew I was holding him in my lap as we bounced along under the starry sky, the cold night air refreshing us after the long ride in the van.

Once I stepped onto the ground beside our cabin, I felt alone again. I carried Chan inside and laid him down in the middle of the mattress. Looking at my boy, I was afraid. The sight of his skin stretched taut over his skull, muscles around his mouth locked tight as his eyes opened

wide, frantically searching for logic when he was moved
and in too much pain—it was all too much for me to bear. I
thought, *Who is this? This is not my child. Where is Chan?* I
didn't recognize this creature, reminiscent of a zombie in
a horror movie. It was only a simple loss of motor control,
but I didn't know that then. Not being able to understand
what he was saying when he was making high-pitched
moans and gesturing with a cramped and flattened fist
was too much for me.

I sat with him briefly till he seemed to sleep. Then
I hurried out the door and down the steps to the open
ground behind our cabin. I ran, feet pounding the hard
dust, shouting at the sky, railing at the heavens, until I
could run no more. Then I leaned over under the darkness and retched. I expelled the fumes of the hospital. I
purged the terror and unknowing that had gripped me all
day. I looked up at the star-spattered sky and yelled into
the night, "I can't stand this! Take him! Take him tonight!
I cannot stand this torture!" I crouched in the dirt, holding my head between my knees, and sobbed.

I walked with heavy limbs to the bench behind our
hut and let the tears run down my cheeks as I peered up
into the sky. Even shy Cam was moved to sit down next
to me and put an awkward hand on my shoulder, offering words intended to comfort. In a rare moment of emotional honesty, I turned and practically yelled at this dear
man, "Have you looked at our son? Just look at him! I
can't even understand him when he speaks!" Cam sat quietly, absorbing my fear, my panic. After some time, when I
seemed to have calmed, he stood up and went to say good
night to Chan.

I still sensed the air of the hospital in my clothes and

on my skin. I still felt the fear of watching Chan shrink into himself throughout the day. I waited, letting the breeze that blew up from the valley carry it all away until I was able to go back to my child. He was sleeping peacefully, and I lay down in my usual spot, between him and Cody, also sleeping, kissed them both good night, and immediately fell asleep.

At one thirty in the morning, Dtaw woke me up and told me to look at Chan. He was breathing slowly, with some effort, open-mouthed and gurgling slightly. As I turned him on his side to alleviate the gurgle, I spoke to Dtaw: "Do you understand what's happening?"

"Yes. I understand."

Chan's breathing seemed unchanged by turning him, so we lifted his head and shoulders from the pillow, holding him between us, our arms around him. And as we watched, ready, yet never ready, he pulled in and pushed out those final raspy breaths, until he was still and quiet and his skin finally shook out his soul for good.

I looked across our son to his father. "Chan has died," I told him.

We didn't cry right away. We were calm as we held him between us and kissed him goodbye. I turned to gently shake Cody awake.

"Cody, honey, wake up. Chan has died." I found myself tempted to say, *I think Chan has died*. I had to force myself to state the fact.

Cody woke up right away and started to cry. "Now I won't have anyone to play 'guys' with," he wailed. "Chan was so fun to play with." I encouraged him to kiss and hug Chan goodbye. I went outside to squat in the dry grass of the rice field lying fallow outside our house, wetting the thirsty soil with my pee. The moon sat fat and orange and huge like half a grapefruit, its curved bottom almost touching the southeast horizon. I thought to myself, *Every time I see a moon like this, I will remember this night.* But I knew even then every time I did a lot of things, I would remember this night.

Back inside our tiny candlelit bedroom, I found Dtaw leaning over Chan's face and howling quietly with grief. Cody and I sat by him, hands resting lightly on his back, and then we all cried, stopping to talk about what we would miss and then crying some more.

Fifteen minutes after Chan's death, Dtaw drove the Land Rover down to the village to get Tahn and to let Cam and Tong know. Soon they returned with their youngest son, Tao, all crying and crowding into the tiny bedroom to say goodbye. Our friends from the village, the other men my children addressed as *Paw*, Father, came up and waited outside by the fire through the night. When it was their turn, they came in too, brushing away the tears that ran stubborn down their cheeks, leaning over to speak to Chan, to wish him well on his journey, touch his head, and say goodbye.

Three-year-old Tahn wasn't crying at all. He continued to smile and tried to work out in his own giggly way the difference between death and sleep. "If I step on his legs, *now* will it hurt?"

After months of being shielded by me and Dtaw and Cody from Tahn's exuberance, Chan was finally safe from injury. Tahn sensed this change and kept asking me about it, smiling impishly yet also wanting to understand. I explained that Chan was dead and even if Tahn stepped on him or kicked him, on purpose or by mistake, it wouldn't hurt. Satisfied, Tahn ran outside to enjoy the rare pleasure of playing with Tao in the midnight dark. He spent the rest of the night coming and going between the fire outside and the room full of grieving family and cooling brother.

DEPARTURE

*I*N THE WEEKS BEFORE, I had envisioned a simple funeral at the forest temple on the mountain where a devout monk lived in solitude. I imagined a solemn and simple ceremony culminating in Chan's cremation over an open pyre. But I soon found out we'd be heading back to my husband's hometown to be with his family and friends. It really didn't matter to me. I was content to do what would be right for Dtaw and his family.

I felt no urge to hurry and pack our things for the funeral. I just wanted to sit with my boy, knowing I would never have another chance to be with him like this. The early morning passed with more silence and weeping. And finally, just before dawn, all four of us crawled under the puffy blue sleeping bag that had warmed Chan these last few months. On either side of him, curved into each other, arms wrapped around one another, around him, we turned to him, as we had so often, and gazed at his beautiful face, wishing him well on his journey. Thinking and sometimes speaking of the immensity of our love for him, of the funny things he'd done, of our grief at losing him and our gratitude for his coming to us at all. "I hope when I die, I can join his herd," Cody said.

Dtaw's brother Giat and Uncle Shoon had arrived before dawn in two pickup trucks. After sunrise, it was time to pack, and with Cody and Tong's help we gathered our things and the men carried them to the truck. When everything was ready, Chan lay alone in the middle of the room, wrapped in the cream-colored flannel sheets a friend from Seattle had given me when we left there, nine months before. Only his head showed. Throughout the night, I had been pulling up his shirt periodically to listen again for his heartbeat, wondering if he might be in a coma rather than dead. As his extremities cooled, the rest of him stayed warm so that I wasn't sure he was dead, but when I waved his helpful uncle away and picked up Chan's long thin body in my arms to carry him into the morning light, my doubts that he might not be dead vanished. This weight in my arms was a corpse, stiff-legged and sallow-faced. His spirit was gone.

I walked down the narrow wooden steps of our house worrying, for the last time, that I would trip and fall with him, but at last knowing I wouldn't hurt him if I did. Instead of heading for the waiting truck, I called to Cody and turned down the dirt track to the horses' pasture. Cody and I talked as we walked. "Why do they always stand by the fence?" he asked. We came to where the five animals stood at the edge of the pasture nearest the house.

"Maybe they just like to be with us, so they are waiting for us," I answered.

I held Chan's head toward the animals, pushing him in close enough for the horses' noses to touch him. They did not hesitate. They came and gently opened their nostrils to his head and hair, breathing him in, as they had done so many times before. I looked at the mother's eyes, wide open and staring straight at me as she never had before, and I told her Chan was gone, but as I spoke, I knew I didn't have to. She looked at me as a mother who understood. When we turned away and trudged back up the hill, I looked down at my baby's sweet face, now appearing more and more dead, and let the sadness well up and the howls issue forth to the gray morning and the emptiness of land and sky. A small part of me stood outside of myself, amazed at the sound, but the rest of me expelled my grief to the universe.

I marveled at the sounds that seemed to issue from the depths of my soul as I carried that small corpse away from the horses and our home. Strangely, those animal cries seemed akin to the roars I'd made when I was birthing Cody, a primal voice, the first time signifying creative power, this time its inverse, yet born from the same deepest part of myself.

For once I did not feel impatience over the long car ride home. Content to sit and hold my child across my lap for the last time, I was in no hurry for the trip to end. I stroked Chan's hair and held Dtaw's arm when he cried. When we got closer to town, we pulled out the phone and Dtaw called his brothers and oldest friends. With each phone call, he broke down and could hardly make himself understood. I was so relieved that Dtaw was able to cry.

I insisted on stopping at the hospital. I wanted to be certain Chan was dead and not in a coma.

"Stop here," I told Uncle Shoon when we reached the emergency room door. I did not want to walk through the big glass doors and waiting room of the main lobby. Dtaw lifted Chan's head and shoulders off my lap so I could climb out from the backseat. Together we managed to pass Chan behind the driver's seat tilted forward, and out the only door on the side of the truck. I carried him into the emergency room. Dtaw and Cody walked beside us. The private hospital was still new and too expensive for this part of the country, so, as usual, the room was empty.

A nurse greeted me with a wide smile that weakened suddenly at the sight of us. She picked up the phone and called for the doctor before she showed me into the same empty room we had come to the day before. I stood in the middle of the room, holding Chan, feeling the strangeness of the floor flat beneath me. No tufts of grass, no hard humps of dirt. The doctor stepped into the room and as soon as he saw Chan, he turned to me, asking, "What would you like me to do?" in a voice gentler than I'd heard him use before.

"I want you to examine him. I want to be sure he is dead."

He gestured that I should lay Chan on the examining table. Lifting the bright eye of the stethoscope to Chan's unmoving chest, the doctor listened. I did not miss the slight shake of the doctor's head. He lifted Chan's left arm and let it flop down. He did this three times (I was surprised—I'd thought that only happened in cartoons). When he pulled up Chan's eyelids and shone his flashlight in, I didn't need to see whether the pupils dilated or not; one look at his eyes showed me Chan's life had left his body. The doctor wanted us to be satisfied, though, so he called in the nurse to take Chan's blood pressure. I watched the mercury fall steadily, no hesitation, both times she checked. The doctor went to find another doctor to complete the examination with a second opinion. When he couldn't locate one, he assured me, in his best medical-school English, "It is not my opinion. It is a fact. He is dead."

We asked about formalin, but upon discovering that it would cause a strong chemical odor, we decided to take care of preserving his body at home. I didn't feel ready to pickle him. We squeezed back into the truck to continue our journey.

Comic relief came when Tahn threw up all over himself and the car dashboard and floor while sitting on Cody's lap in front. Dtaw and I were pinned down under Chan's body, so we couldn't help. Cody and Uncle Shoon had to handle it themselves. Cody had held Tahn in his lap for the whole three-hour journey to the capital.

For the last half hour of the trip we all tried to distract Tahn from his car sickness by pointing out cars and trucks and water buffaloes and cows in the distance.

"Umboh! Umboh!" Uncle Shoon kept calling, imitating the sound of a cow mooing. It worked until we were two blocks from home and Tahn threw up again.

When we pulled up in front of the house, Dtaw's mom and sister came out, sobbing, and Dtaw broke down again. By the time I carried Chan to the low wooden table they had readied for him in the center of the living room, everyone's tears had stopped.

PART 6

FUNERAL

"*S*UWOY MAK! *KEU BAO DTAI!*" (So beautiful! As if he were still alive!) the elders murmured as they came close to pay their respects, touching Chan's sleeve or straightening his collar. They were puzzled that his body didn't seem to be hardening at all. By afternoon, my mother-in-law, along with one or two of the other elders, even took his head between her gnarled fingers to give it a shake. Her hands had the strength needed for a mother to raise six children, but this time she held Chan's head gently between her fingers, curved like talons, as she shook it from side to side, testing the softness of his neck. The elders kept saying they'd never seen a corpse, even a child's, that didn't harden quickly. There was some discussion as to whether he was actually dead, despite my report of the doctor's examination of him that morning. They had less faith in Western medicine than I did. Death was too much the realm of spirits for doctors to have much authority.

Dtaw's older brother Pong, the middle-aged abbot with plump shoulders emerging from the umber robes of his vocation, officiated over the proceedings. In Thailand, funerals are always in the dead person's home. The first floor of the house, which had plenty of room for a coffin and guests, was cleared of all furniture except the low heavy table of polished wood that often served as a sofa or bed for family members to nap or sit on, to chat or watch TV, or to have a massage. During a funeral, it became the bier.

Pong sat opposite me, next to Chan that first day, leaning over him, tenderly examining his face and hands and repeating, "He's sleeping quietly," refusing to let him be put in the coffin just yet.

To add to the mystery of this look of aliveness, Chan continued to pee throughout the day, so that we had to keep changing the bedding under him until we finally just took off his pants and put a plastic bag and towel under him and a blanket over him. Pong kept putting off the hour to lay him in the coffin, which was fine with me.

While Chan might have looked soft and alive, his torso had been cold since midmorning. By sundown, I knew without any doubt that he was dead, even if no one else was completely sure. His foot was arched unnaturally into a stiff point like an awkward ballerina's, and by the end of the day his jaw seemed stiff. As darkness fell, I bent low over his face to kiss his smooth forehead and rest my cheek on his soft skin for almost the last time. The sour sweet scent of decay assured me he was gone. I told Pong it was time to put him in the long wooden box that Dtaw's uncle had built for him that morning. Pong examined him again and agreed.

I was pleased with the hi-tech coffin we had chosen. There had been two options—a traditional box that would be shut tight to keep the smell of decay sealed inside, or the electric coffin with a cooling unit. We chose the electric option. Colorful, garish, painted in bright gold, red, and green carved flowers and goddesses, it was, in essence, a very large freezer into which we would slide the lidless wooden box Chan was in. He would be slowly frozen over a few days and then thawed the night before the cremation (to save on coal). A small window in the top of the coffin allowed me to check on him whenever I wanted. There was even a light to illuminate his angelic face. I loved watching him so peaceful and beautiful, a face so much easier to look at than the one tortured by pain and loss of brain function I had watched the night before.

Chan's friends in the neighborhood and his brothers expected that they would shave their heads and take monks' robes for the day, the custom for boys and men when a family member dies. When Pong had had time to consider it, he decided that that custom was reserved for only adult deaths. As the little boys gathered around me eagerly awaiting the answer, and I delivered the news, their disappointment rose in silent looks and shuffling feet. Cody's eyes stayed focused on the floor, not daring to meet my gaze, for fear of too much emotion welling up if he did, I supposed.

Over the three days of the funeral, a dozen or so of Dtaw's closest friends and one of his old uncles—the carpenter who'd built not only Chan's casket, but also his crib—worked together to construct the spirit house. Tradition required that Chan have, at his cremation, a house the size of a child's playhouse that represented the home Chan would have in his next life. Building it from wood donated by friends from the lumberyard, they sawed and measured and drilled and hammered and drank and talked far into the night. They decorated it with intricate paper cutouts, snipped while they smoked cigarettes and sipped whiskey and soda, working with utmost concentration, interrupted by only a joke and a laugh now and then. Dtaw's uncle even fashioned two horse heads out of a banana leaf stem to adorn the roof of the house like the decorations on top of the temples.

There were abundant flowers given by Dtaw's eldest brother, and funeral wreaths of waxy blooms from schools and local businesses, and tray after tray of delicious foods, each day made by a team of women who set up an outdoor kitchen and worked all hours turning out hot, nourishing meals. Pots of sweet homemade soy milk boiled in the yard and fresh doughnuts sizzled in oil.

We stayed up past midnight every night, talking and laughing and sharing funny stories and drawing comfort from each other. It was good to have people there around the clock. Each night Tong and Cam and Dtaw brought out a huge pile of blankets and pillows so everyone could sleep on the floor near Chan's coffin. And twice every day, in the early morning and in the evening, a group of monks came from all of the different temples in town to chant and provide the structure we needed for mourning.

Chanting is a soothing experience that seems to quiet the mind; I was grateful for that. And in Thai culture there is such a strong belief in karma—beyond a sense of punishment and reward, more of a rational yet unintelligible order to all events—that everyone was quite certain Chan's death was something that could not have been avoided, and for that reason wasn't some cruel and unbelievable tragedy.

"He brought his illness with him," and, "He was

meant to finish this life early," were phrases I heard over and over. Although I wasn't sure I agreed, it did make it a little easier to think that all of it was part of some sensible order to the universe. And just as I would have at home, I often heard, "He's no longer suffering," which was the thing that I was most grateful for.

I would much rather, however, have had him suffering a little bit and still be alive.

~~~

FIRE

~~~

*I*T WAS LATE AFTERNOON ON DECEMBER 24, 2004, midwinter, but warm enough for me to be comfortable in a loose white cotton shirt and black silk pants, traditional colors for mourning. The cremation ceremony at the temple was over, and Chan's body was burning in the huge brick oven inside the crematorium, its chimney like a cylindrical church spire. A few of our closest friends stayed and sat with me and Dtaw amid the scores of folding chairs still set up around the crematorium, or *mayn*. The word for crematorium in English is not right. It sounds too industrial and practical. Nowadays, when outdoor funeral pyres are only found in remote Thai villages, almost every temple compound includes a *mayn* as one if its central buildings. The architecture is in the style of the rest of the temple, without the brightly colored ornamentation of the largest temple building that houses the Buddha image. Bright white walls lean in toward a steeply peaked roof, graceful lines sweeping heavenward with steps that lead up from three sides to the small area in front of the metal door of the oven. The oven itself is a large room with rails like train tracks leading to the center. The tracks make it easier to slide the coffin in and shut the heavy metal door. The smooth cement floor in front affords enough room for the coffin and a dozen or so mourners at a time as they file by, laying flowers and incense on the body. The *mayn* at this temple, one of seven in the town, was large enough so that we and all eighteen members of Dtaw's immediate family could stand on one set of steps and stare solemnly into Dtaw's cousin's camera for the funeral photos.

Dtaw's family had chosen this temple for Chan's cremation because it was where Dtaw's father's ashes were kept. His grandparents' ashes were at the temple at the end of their street. This temple was farther out of town, across from his family's farm, but it was often visited by one of the most highly revered monks in Thailand.

The ceremony had started just after dawn, with chanting at our house before the procession to the temple behind the oxcart and pickup truck that carried the coffin, friends and uncles and cousins packed in tight around it, still holding Chan by keeping their hands on the wooden box. Now at midafternoon, most of the other guests had gone home. We felt no desire to leave. What was there for us at home? Our friends An and It and their young son Phu sat with us. Dtaw's lifelong friend and neighbor Jan and his wife Lek stayed too. All of them talked together with an ease I rarely saw in my American world, where a certain awkwardness seemed to pervade social situations, especially funerals. But the people I knew in Dtaw's world seemed at ease with their fellow beings. And a funeral was a sad but normal event. That afternoon they chatted not about Chan, but about old friends' misadventures or where to buy the best shiitake mushrooms or mountain bike tires. I listened some, but my mind and eyes were on the heavy door behind which my son's body was slowly turning to ash. I wanted to go up and look, but I was afraid the people around me would try to stop me. I wasn't sure I had the courage anyway.

I got up to visit the outhouse across the temple yard behind the *mayn*. My sandals crunched over the yellow blades of dead bamboo leaves littering the ground and speckled gold in the afternoon sun filtering through the treetops. As I walked, I determined that I would look in on my way back. I hoped that if I cut around to the side stairs and stepped quietly enough, I might not be noticed until I reached the door. It wasn't that I didn't want people to know what I was doing. It was that I was afraid they would come at me, loud with caring protest, interrupting with their concern the silence of my isolation.

I lifted my tired legs up the cement steps and thought, *Do I really want to do this?* I told myself it was not Chan. It was an empty rotting corpse, fit only for burning or burying. Convinced, and refusing to be intimidated by my own fears, I fixed my gaze at the top of the steps and steeled myself for what I would see after I reached that spot. I stood before the solid metal door, the mechanics of its spoked wheel and levers like the door on the hatch of a submarine. I leaned in toward the thick glass that covered the small window in the center and looked. Much to my relief, because of the small size of the hole, I saw only dancing gold flames and nothing else.

I was exhaling with relief and turning away when the old man whose job it was to tend the fire all night came hobbling up the stairs. His gray hair was cut close to his scalp and the stubble of his whiskers prickled along the flesh of his loose jowls. His eyes seemed sleepy and dull, but as the keeper of the fire, he had spotted me as I crept up to the door.

He spoke to me in the local dialect: "Come, I'll open it up so you can really see." He spoke without adding any of the usual terms of endearment an old person uses with someone my age—*little mouse, small one,* customary syllables that would have softened his tone. He spoke to me directly, without the slightest hint of pity. I was grateful for this. I dutifully returned to the door, and he leaned his stocky body back, pulling against the weight of the lever. As he did, it gave way and swung open, splitting the top half from the bottom and affording an unobstructed view of my son's burning corpse.

Very little was recognizable. The skull which I looked for at the top of the oblong blackened pile must have crumbled to ash already because I couldn't make it out. The only parts I thought I could recognize were two very long bones, which at first, because of the way they stuck out perpendicular from the body, I thought to be his upper arm bones, but which I realized because of their size must have been his thigh bones. I had seen enough, I thought, but the old man walked a few steps away and picked up a blackened, long-handled trident missing the middle tine. He then lifted it and poked it into the fire to jab what must have been Chan's back and turn the body over.

I backed away and turned around as this part of his body seemed to have more charred intact matter than the rest of it. I feared I would see some bit that still looked like Chan. When I saw bits of red where the points of the fire tool poked in, I foolishly thought it was blood, but later I realized it was probably his favorite red polyester soccer shirt I had dressed him in for the funeral, refusing to burn.

I joined my friends, glad I hadn't been too disturbed by the sight and glad they didn't reproach me for going up. Chan's friend Phu, who had been born just a month after Chan, went skipping boldly up the stairs and peeked through the hole and came down telling his mom brightly, "It smells like a barbecue!" She shushed him and I tried to tell her not to worry. I had already noticed that. Indeed, that was what had come to my mind when I saw the burning corpse: a very large and overdone barbecue. Strange, I always thought the smell of a burning body would be worse than that, but it wasn't.

~~~

REMAINS

~~~

*T*HE NEXT MORNING BEFORE SUNRISE, Mei Ya stood in the street under our window and called out her son's name: "Dtaw! Dtaw!" The insistent staccato shouts rose above the ragged cries of the roosters and through the mosquito net around the bed where Dtaw, our two remaining sons, and I slept. She hurried us until we were all crammed, limp and bleary-eyed, into our cousin's car. Stoic relatives crowded into the bed of the family pickup truck to follow us out of the village and down the misty road past mango and tamarind farms.

At the temple we uncrimped ourselves from the car and stepped through the darkness up the steps of the crematorium. Yesterday's firekeeper and another old stubble-scalped man came up from where they sat at a small fire in the dirt. All night they had tended the fire so that it would consume my child's body by daybreak. One of them opened the thick door, sliding out the iron bed that now held glowing coals and nothing I could recognize as the thirty-two-pound boy in a glossy-red soccer suit under a mound of paper flowers I had pushed into the massive oven the day before. The men shoveled the embers onto a piece of corrugated tin which they carried to the ground and doused with water.

The whole family crouched down in the dark and chill of early morning and began to pick through the wet ashes. In the glow of the flashlights the old men held over our shoulders, the treasures of bone, small gray shards, were sometimes indistinguishable from the lumps of wet coal.

My brother-in-law, the monk, handed me a slender stick of bamboo, split halfway up the middle like long takeout chopsticks, so I could avoid burning my fingers on any coals that weren't wet. I wiped the wet ashes from my fingertips and set to work with Cody, Tahn, Dtaw, and the rest of the family. The bits of bone mixed in with the ash were small and light, and I thought of a bird's skeleton. There were a few larger ones, but as the family dug through them to choose which to keep and which to throw into the jungle, I didn't take time to identify them.

We dropped the ones we wanted to keep into hollow sections of banana tree trays that the men had cut by removing the inner layers of the tree's trunk. As we worked, the old men picked up these fragments and rinsed them in a bucket of water before putting them in the clear plastic pickle jar Mei Ya had brought.

When we had enough pieces of bone in the jar, the old men's hands formed the wet ashes into the rough shape of a human. They stuck small yellow candles into the figure at places prescribed by tradition. Mei Ya brought out a Tupperware box of coins and we distributed them over the figure. Someone said he hoped Chan would be rich in his next life. Cody said, "I hope he can buy a lot of horses." They all spoke in the local dialect, the one my children spoke before they learned English. It's closer to Laotian than Thai and easier for me to understand. It is the language of home.

Ushered into the high-ceilinged temple, open on all sides to the morning air, we knelt before the monks seated on the platform and joined in the Buddhist chant that begins every one of the countless ceremonies I have attended in Thailand. It was the same one we chanted with family and neighbors to welcome my babies into this world and the one we chanted to send my father-in-law into the next when I was pregnant with Cody.

"*Namo Tassa Baghavato, Arahato . . .*" In resonating vibrations, the monks droned the Pali words that honor the blessed self-awakened Buddha, and we chanted after them in turns.

Three-year-old Tahn refused to sit on the mat with his feet pointed politely away from the Buddha image at the front of the room. "You want a piece of me?" he kept threatening before he tried his Thai boxing moves on me. Cody, a planet out of orbit now without its sun, found staying conscious for this final ritual of death impossible and, only a couple of hours after waking up, put his head on my lap and slept hard.

The night after we collected Chan's ashes, I was sighing when Cody spoke up.

"Mom, you know that's getting kind of annoying."

"What?" I asked, shaken out of my thoughts.

"You keep sighing. You started the day before Chan died. You keep saying, *Chan, Chan, Chan,* and sighing."

I thought about this and then said, "I miss Chan every minute. Do you?"

"Every second," he replied.

* * *

The next morning, when we had all gathered back at the temple for the final ceremony of the funeral, Pong spoke to me: "Little Kay, I want to tell you that last night while my brother monks chanted at the temple, the smell of a body came to them. They looked around for a dead gecko or rat, but found nothing. Afterward, they realized it must be Chan coming to listen to the chanting. They said to him, *All right now, go along now, go back to where you belong*, and the smell immediately vanished. They told me the story and asked if Chan liked chanting. I said yes, of course."

I listened in respectful silence to his story before waiting to speak. When I did, I held my palms pressed together in front of my chest and cast my eyes down at the ground, as is required when addressing a monk, even your brother-in-law.

"Chan used to love to go to listen to the chanting at the temple when he was little," I said, "and would keep telling me when they weren't yet chanting, *Make them sing, Mama. Make them sing!*" Curious if the smell of the smoke of the cremation fire could carry the five miles across town to Pong's hilltop temple, I asked him if the monks smelled a burning body or a rotting body. A rotting one, he replied.

We scattered Chan's ashes and bits of bone two days later. After breakfast, Mei Ya handed me a large silver bowl, intricately laced with images of fertility and the cosmos. Part of her dowry, now it held the petals of the traditional nine different kinds of flowers, colorful, fragrant, and reminiscent of heavenly beings. We walked to the river's edge at the end of our street where a narrow, wooden long-tail boat waited. The captain held out his hand to help me step onto the open craft with his usual wordless grace. I set the bowl on the bow next to the bundle of ashes wrapped in white cloth and jar of bones. A bouquet of marigolds stood at the prow where the boatman had set them, fresh from his garden, his daily offering to the river spirits.

We motored upriver through the morning mist and sunshine until the driver cut the engine, and we floated downriver. Despite so many relatives in the boat (fifteen in all), the ride was silent. Dtaw and I untied the plain cotton cloth that held the ashes, poured the bone shards from the jar onto them, and covered it all with the flower petals. Cody and Tahn and Jew helped Dtaw and Cam and me lift the bundle over the side to tilt the last tangible elements of their brother into the swirling brown water. The gray dust of his ashes floated and shimmered in the sun on the surface before the water swallowed them. We dropped the cloth and empty plastic jar in too.

As the boat slid downriver, each person threw a handful of petals toward the place where we'd scattered Chan's ashes. The colorful petals spread out over the surface of the brown river and floated and followed us as we drifted.

When we came to the steps in front of our street, the captain pulled the boat up gently against the rocks. I turned to look back at the wide river with the winding trail of flower petals, a long curve of color surging toward the faraway sea. It reminded me of the Naga, the serpent that was believed to inhabit the waters of the Mekong and that once coiled itself under the Lord Buddha during a thunderstorm, spreading its hood over His head to keep

Him dry as He sought enlightenment. Chan loved the stories of this revered spirit, Payanak. It was the name he'd chosen for our colt.

PART 7

BACK TO THE MOUNTAIN

~~~

A WEEK LATER WE ARRIVED BACK AT THE CABIN. I looked across the barren fields in the valley to the distant hills like earthen waves where elephants and tigers roamed free. Only a few days before I had thought it was beautiful here. But now, without Chan, it felt empty and desolate.

The day we arrived, Dtaw, normally busy cutting back growth or planting trees or herbs or building a stand for a water jar, sat alone on the bench overlooking the valley. When I sat down next to him, he was silent for a while before saying, "It's not the same now."

I put my arm around him and leaned my head on his shoulder. "I know."

It was as if we had had some worthy project we were engaged in: making Chan well. Everything was part of that: the rainwater we drank, the fresh vegetables we ate, the horses we loved to watch and ride, even the hawks and eagles that swooped close enough for Chan to shout out their names. Where before we dwelt in abundance and possibility, now we could see only emptiness.

* * *

That night when I came into the candlelit bedroom to undress for bed, Cody said, "Mom, does it hurt when you die?"

"It could hurt a lot, but we were lucky because Chan's death was mostly slow and gentle. I don't think he had much pain at the very end."

"Then why did he cry?"

"I imagine he was sad at leaving us. Or maybe it's some physiological thing. I don't know. Maybe he was crying at all the sadness in the world."

I thought about Chan all the time. Getting into our bed, lying on the spot where he spent his last night and drew his last breaths, I always felt him near me.

Cody talked about him all the time after he died. Sometimes he said, "I miss Chan," or, "I wish Chan didn't have to die." But more often he remembered. "Every time I smell this soap, it reminds me of the day before Chan died," or, "It's too bad because our friends will ride in the back of the pickup, and Chan would have loved that."

When Dtaw sat silent on the bench, shoulders hunched with despair, I told him our lives would be like that for a while: sad. I hoped I wasn't telling him not to complain. When he hugged me and I started to cry, I hoped I wasn't stopping him from crying. But I couldn't hold back my tears.

Every night for weeks after Chan's death, Dtaw and I both woke up around one thirty a.m. The light, the moon, the stars, our mood sometimes seemed to suggest another time of night, but when we flicked on the flashlight or lit the lamp, the clock always said one thirty, the time Chan died. One morning as we lay together in the darkness, we talked about the moment Chan died.

"How do you think he woke me up?" Dtaw asked me. "With his *jit*?" (Pali for heart-mind.)

"Yes, I think so, honey. He couldn't move his hands, could he? He couldn't even open his eyes, but he knew what was happening." Dtaw and I marveled that, although Chan couldn't control any part of his body, he could still wake up Dtaw from a deep sleep.

We were sure Chan knew it was time to leave us.

"It upsets me that Cody didn't get to take up monk's robes for Chan's funeral. I don't know why Pong decided that," I began to complain.

"I think it was perfect. I think we did it all just right for Chan," Dtaw said firmly.

He was right. It was all just right. There was no sense in doubting any of it. Chan had the best possible end to his life, strong and hopeful and still asserting his right to live right to the last seconds. He never gave up. He never stopped living until he had no choice. He complained loudly about not being able to run or stand and about his pain, but he didn't stop fighting.

I think now I did the right thing. All the times that I wanted to tell him, *You're dying, honey. You can give up now. The cancer is winning. Just rest. Have some ice cream,* I never thought about what his reaction would have been, only that I was afraid that mentioning death would hasten his. I never realized that he would have probably laughed in my face and asked for more bitter vegetable juice.

He was not confused about his life. He knew he had the right to fight as hard as he wanted and never give up before he had to. He died knowing he had lived fully and fought his hardest. If I had been honest with him about my fears of his death, seeing him laugh at them would have helped me see them for what they were: only fears, not reality.

The reality was that he was not dying. He was living. He was living fully in the present and did so every moment until his last breath.

A few days after he died, I looked up into the blue sky over the house and saw an enormous eagle circling overhead. I watched its graceful arcs climbing upward, riding the updrafts from the valley far below. It soared higher until it became little more than a speck, higher than I'd ever watched a bird fly. Then it headed to the north and soared farther upward until it disappeared from view. I thought about how Chan loved eagles and how I'd never seen one spend such a long time above our house. I thought about all the indigenous cultures that read signs of the spirit world in nature, in animals and birds and plants. And how odd it is that my newly developed Western culture is arrogant enough to laugh at these ancient views. What do we know in our youth and logic?

It was then that I began to look up, to look up for him every day.

A month after Chan's death, the January wind cooled my face as I biked over the rough dirt road toward home. I heard the rhythmic *thunk, thunk, thunk* of the rice pounder and saw Tong's muscular form stepping on and off the seesaw of the tree trunk to pump it up and down into a bowl, four feet deep and sunk into the earth. Tong walked the mile up the hill from her village every day to bring fresh garlic or greens from her garden or some sweet rice treat from her kitchen. Now, with Chan gone, she knew better than I did that we still needed her.

As I biked over the crest of the hill, Tahn saw me and untangled himself from the old grass mat he was playing on and came running barefoot over the warm earth and dead broken grass to meet me, a big smile lighting up his face. I don't know where I'd have been without his zest for life, undaunted even with all the sadness of Chan's death. He told me to change my shoes and clothes so I could help with the pounding.

Side by side, Tong and I pounded the rice, leaning together on the wooden rail for support, combining our weight to step in unison onto the end of the log, letting the heavy mallet at the other end come crashing down onto the golden grains. After a while Tong let me pump alone while she separated the rice from the chaff.

It was hard to get the rhythm right, not letting my leg get banged on the pedal's upswing as the mallet at the other end hit the rice at the bottom of the mortar. I let myself go easy, let myself be awkward, not pushing for perfection, knowing the right rhythm would come of its own accord. As my legs began to tire, Tong put a pile of threshed grains onto a round bamboo tray. She gave this to me to pick out the few grains that didn't get pounded to put back in the mortar. The rice felt delightfully cool and dry under our fingers as Tahn and I hunted for the grains, golden against the tan of the threshed. One by one we picked them out and set them aside to return to the mortar.

I was always fascinated by the way the care for a single grain of rice was so important in Thai culture. There was something about the action of taking just a few grains and carefully placing them back with thousands of others that so clearly mattered. It did matter. The rice that we eat is made up of single grains. I learned by living with people who raise rice that when you are not mindful of every grain of rice, you are dishonoring a whole constellation of beings: the farmers and buffaloes who worked to till the land, the people who planted the seedlings, the tiny organisms that fertilized the mud, the women who rose before dawn to pound the hulls off the day's supply. When a villager sees rice, he sees the sun warming the earth and the clouds giving rain. He is careful with each grain.

It felt good to do such simple physical tasks each day: knitting, walking, chopping, pounding. The stitches, strokes, and steps, like pulses, seemed to keep me on the earth, a security I might not have so easily found in a suburban house or city apartment, where my life would have required more of my own directive.

There, a month after Chan's death, I could simply do, without thinking. The fire had to be lit, the rice had to be threshed and cooked and served, the bedding had to be aired and reassembled, the floor swept. Perhaps it would have been the same back in the US, but because of the breezy skies over horses and birds and bugs, it was the place I needed to be. I knew this all along. I had wanted to bring Chan here because I knew it would be the best place for him to get well, but I also knew it would be the best place for him to die, the best place to grieve.

For the first time since I was a very little girl, I was sure that I was in exactly the right place. I belonged there. I knew that whatever I was doing, it was a kind of incubation, recovering from a year and a half of emotional rollercoasting, vertigo, and heartbreak. I allowed myself to be quiet and nurtured, not try to do anything useful at all.

I found it a restful place in my head to be after so many years of beating myself up for not striving enough, not making enough money, not challenging myself enough. I knew after Chan's death that I'd been challenged enough to last a long time.

I liked having the creatures around. The horses kept us on our toes, shooing them away from the house and the rain jars; the wood mice kept us from getting messy in the kitchen; the birds reminded us of the infinite—and it all reminded me that where there is life, there is always birth at one end and death at the other.

It was the usual time of night when I woke up, an hour and a half after midnight. The moon shone bright behind the tree. My sons and husband slept soundly. I tried to wake Dtaw up to talk. He grunted, laid his palm on my cheek, and continued to sleep.

I lay and worried about how it all started. Those chemicals he took in so young when I had asthma during pregnancy? So much albuterol in the womb when he was so tiny? I struggled with the knowledge that I would never know. It didn't matter, though. It was over, and we were left with so much sadness and so much love that felt like only a memory, like thirsty hands cupped, remembering icy clear water and long cool drafts.

One hundred and five days after Chan's death, Dtaw and Tahn and I were riding the motorcycle under the hot bright sun through the streets of town. Tahn was delighted to be squeezed between the two of us, his blond and brown curls and his daddy's long black and gray strands twisting together in the wind. He said, "That'd be cool, Mama, if you and me and Jew and Cody and Chan were flying in the sky."

"Yes, that would be, honey. Do you think Chan is already flying up there?" I asked.

"Yeah, look!" he said with happy certainty, and he craned his head back and pointed his chubby arm straight up into the blue as if he could see his big brother.

I do feel these days that he's still with us, watching us, maybe guiding us along.

He has moved us a few degrees up. I get mired in my own travails less now than I did before. I don't squint down into the blackness of my own mind so much anymore.

Now I try to look up. I try to see the sky.

Acknowledgments

I would like to express my gratitude to the following people. As of this writing, these are the names I can remember. If yours does not appear here and you were part of this journey, please know I am deeply grateful to you as well.

Chan's father Dtaw for teaching me how to fight for what matters most.

Cody, Tahn, Jew, Jum, Mei Ya, Cam, and Tong for so much love.

Mom for teaching me to cherish. Dave and Vivian for knowing when we needed them. Thomas for showing up without asking.

My Stonecoast mentors Deb Marquart, Suzanne Strempek Shea, Ted Deppe, and Rick Bass, with extra thanks to Rick for reading so many pages before I could see where it all was going. Robin Talbot, Justin Tussing, and Matt Jones for their hard work, support, and good humor. My Stonecoast classmates, especially Jenny O'Connell, Tiffany Joslin, and Heather Wilson for all the moral support and dancing. Carter Walker for seeing beauty, and Melanie Viets for the same and for the quiet. My Stonecoast writing group—Kris Millard, Sophie Nelson, Mary Katherine Spain, Bill Stauffer, and Ryan Brod—for their close readings, honesty, and encouragement. A special thank you to Ryan for letting me cry but not letting me quit.

My editors Ann Hood and Johnny Temple for their skill and patience and for knowing that people need stories like this. My book designer Lucian Burg for his generosity, sensitivity, and artistic vision. And Tris Coburn for believing in this early on and for advising me on all things literary agent.

Humble thanks to our family and neighbors in Thailand for watching and holding it all with patience and kindness. Our community in Seattle for working together to support us without even being asked. The nurses and doctors at Seattle Children's Hospital for their compassion and expertise. My Loeipittayakom, University of Southern Maine, and Portland Adult Education faculty families for taking me on when I was still so sad. My co-counseling communities in Portland and Seattle for reminding me over and over that healing takes more time and tears than we would like.

And thanks to all my incredible friends. Cynthia for seeing the story from the start. Sherry and Hannah for bringing sunshine when we needed it. Payne for saying yes. Lenna for being there through the hardest parts. Lynn and Amy for still listening after all these years. Kecia for always laughing with me. Christina and Deirdre for knowing what we needed, especially when we were lost. Amy, John, Deb, and Dave for so much I can't even begin to say. Julia for being my friend—always. Peter for all the love, education, and support. Marcella for being real. Sharie for Trauma Incident Reduction miracles. And my Big Dreams group—Layne, Anne, Cathy, and Deb—it worked!